Cater or Die
A Step-by-Step Plan For Doubling Your Catering Profits

by
Michael Attias

www.RestaurantCateringSoftware.com

TABLE OF CONTENTS

PREFACE

WHO THE HELL IS MICHAEL ATTIAS, AND WHY SHOULD I LISTEN TO HIM?

CATER OR DIE

Before we embark on this journey, I want to thank you for downloading this book. You have many options when it comes to how you invest your time, especially the time you invest building your business.

I don't want to waste your time! Before we go any further, I want you to know this book was not written by a professional writer or someone who saw an "opportunity" in the catering business.

This book was written by someone just like you. The introduction will spell out my background and more of what to expect, but I wanted you to know I started a 104 seat restaurant in 1992 just outside of Nashville, Tennessee, and took the catering from zero to over a million dollars a year.

Exhibit 1 is a copy of a letter from my CPA certifying my sales the last year before I sold my restaurant.

Now where I come from, the banks don't give you extra money on your deposit slip if you worked hard to make it. I was able to grow my catering sales to the top 1% of all restaurants by learning from others.

It's time for me to give back. If you are open to learning from my successes and failures, you'll walk away with a ton of practical, low cost ideas to help you build your own catering sales. Many of these ideas you can

MEMORANDUM

DATE: May 11, 2006

TO: Whom It May Concern

FROM: Michael Roberts, Partner

RE: Oink, Inc. d/b/a Corky's Ribs & Bar-B-Q 2005 Catering Sales

I have personally worked with Michael Attias, Vice President of Oink, Inc.'s Corky's Ribs & Bar-B-Q franchise in Brentwood, Tennessee and prepared their books and income tax returns since 1995.

For calendar year 2005 the restaurant reported on their federal income tax return full service catering sales of $324,749.43 and drop-off/self-service catering sales of $679,810.14 for total catering sales of $1,004,559.50.

These sales figures were generated from a single unit with seating of 104 in the main dining room.

[signature]

1801 West End Avenue • Palmer Plaza Suite 900 • Nashville, Tennessee 37203
Voice 615.312.9050 / Fax 615.312.9100 / www.horne-llp.com

EXHIBIT 1

put into action immediately.

In case you're wondering why I'm giving away information others have paid me $5,000 a day to learn or attended high priced Boot Camps, it's simple.

CATER OR DIE

I know 90% of your fellow restaurant owners, some even competitors, will read this book, find it interesting, even get excited, but do nothing.

This book is for the other 10%; the movers, shakers and doers. Nothing happens until you take action. Reading this book makes you an action taker.

I'm betting you'll be one of the 10% tired of struggling to build your catering sales. My message will resonate with you.

You'll either go about on your own trying to figure out how to replicate my "catering system", or choose to work with me and the good folks at my company Restaurant Catering Systems.

Either way, I'm good with that.

So grab a cup of coffee, lock the door and let's get started!

To You And Your Restaurant's Success!

Michael Attias
President
Restaurant Catering Systems
615-831-1676
www.RestaurantCateringSoftware.com

INTRODUCTION

CATER OR DIE

My very first job was in the restaurant business – the Loft in Memphis, Tennessee. It was September of 1981, and I actually had to show up in a dress shirt and tie to interview for the dishwashing position. If it had not been for my "in" with a friend who was a busboy there, my application would have been lost in the thick stack.

I lasted a week as a dishwasher before my lousy cleansing of pots and pans landed me a promotion to busboy. I've been moving my way up the restaurant ladder ever since. Luckily, I owe most of it to my abilities, not my inabilities.

During college I waited tables for a friend's father, Don Pelts, at a restaurant called Corky's Bar-B-Q in Memphis, Tennessee. In hindsight, it was a ground floor opportunity. But at the time, the quick cash and getting out of school to get a "real job" was my priority.

I'm sure you've heard similar words from your staff. They are making a big mistake with that thinking. Working in a restaurant is a real job that pays real money and has done quite well by me. While at The Loft I had the opportunity to put together a grand opening promotion for our new bar addition.

At Corky's, Don gave me the reins to create a gift certificate promotion and create their original model for shipping ribs and barbecue across country via Federal Express.

It took getting out of the restaurant business to discover the opportunities that I had overlooked.

After college I spent two years selling archive storage. An archive storage company stores boxes of old files and records for companies and retrieves them when needed. It was a difficult, unexciting selling experience. Most people were happy to have their records rot in a damp, musty basement or mini-storage. Add to that my sales training in cold call selling, and you can see why I only made it two years. I'll discuss cold call selling later in the book and how to never have to make a cold call again.

Two years into my after college "real job", I was at a crossroad in my life. Just having bought a house and recently married, I desired a more lucrative opportunity. I considered selling printing and chemicals ; businesses my father and father-in-law were in at the time .

Ultimately, the restaurant siren pulled me back in, and I found myself back at Corky's Bar-B-Q. But I had a game plan. I waited tables at night to pay my bills and worked in the kitchen during the day for free to learn the operation.

Corky's was franchising and I knew that I could get one of my customers to back me on one of the first franchises. Ask a hundred qualified customers and surely one will write the check. Cold call selling taught me that eventually you'll get a yes. In 1992 I think it was my 47th prospect, and his wife, that came in one day from just outside Nashville, Tennessee, and sat in my station for a barbecue fix. They pulled out an ad about a Corky's Bar-B-Q franchising opportunity in the Nashville, Tennessee market and asked me about it. By the end of their meal, Bill and Salter Rackley were my new best friends. A week later we met in Nashville and we finalized the backing.

To this day, I consider the million dollar plus investment in that store my greatest tip. What was even more remarkable is that I had never managed a restaurant before, not to mention built one from scratch.

My two restaurant jobs taught me a ton about great customer service, producing incredible food and focusing on a clean operation. But was there more?

Do you remember your first meal in a restaurant? For me it was May of 1971. I had just graduated kindergarten earlier that day and my parents gave me a bright red Bounce-A-Roo as my gift. For those of you who do not remember the Bounce-A-Roo, it's a large ball with ears that you ride like a horse, jumping your way

INTRODUCTION

across the yard.

Today, I'd end up on the ground or in a chiropractor's office.

The giant ball pails in comparison to the Big Wheel. If you see me in person, remember to ask me about the time my brother Oliver, at the ripe old age of 5, road his Big Wheel 2 miles away from home on a busy street. Guess who was in trouble? I guess my parents did consider me my brother's keeper.

Now back to my big meal out. We went to a Chinese restaurant. The only thing I remember were the egg rolls with the bright orange sweet and sour sauce. Unfortunately, I didn't heed my dad's warning to avoid the spicy yellow mustard. French's it wasn't.

Minus vacations, I think I can count the times I went out to dinner at a restaurant during my early grade school years on a hand or two.

Today, my kids Jerrod and Jordyn surpass that number any week they spend with me.

Used to be that opening a restaurant, any restaurant, was a ticket to making money, assuming you weren't poisoning your customers and didn't own a roach farm. As you well know, as a market matures, the competition increases and the need to differentiate is more crucial.

I have helped thousands of restaurants, independents and chains tackle the challenges of increased competition and decreasing sales and profits. Once you establish a catering foothold, it is far more difficult to be dethroned than from your dining room business.

As consumers, we tend to be fickle. We want to try the new place. Maybe a server pissed us off and... "we'll never go back there again." Whew! I wish everyone in America had to either spend two years in military service or waiting tables. Then they'd know.

Catering, on the other hand, is a relationship business. Above the quality of the food and more important than being "in", is a need for a business to be served: last minute orders, billing, accommodating for the lone vegan in the bunch, etc.

What if you haven't built a firm catering position in your marketplace? My advice to you is get busy now. The first settlers out West were able to stake claim to the best mines. The ones that followed were stuck panning for gold. And the ones that followed them were probably bussing tables at the local saloon.

I once received an email from a subscriber of my e-letter, The Restaurant Marketing Minute, telling me about all the money he had sunk into his restaurant…the fact he hadn't pulled out a dime…cleaned out his 401k… mortgaged his house to the hilt…had two girls to put through school…

He asked me to help him for free and ended the letter by telling me that if I didn't help him for free, I was a charlatan like all the other "snake oil salesmen".

The question I asked him was, "What have you done with all the free advice I've delivered in your In Box for the last couple of years?"

"Nothing", he said.

Well, even without a marketing budget, you can still market. Last time I checked, local calls were still free. If his place isn't busy, then surely he has time to knock on doors instead of me.

I fired the guy! I took him out of my database, and told him not to bother even trying to order anything from me. I don't need his money. Harsh? No. I have no tolerance for those unwilling to help themselves.

Cater or Die! was not created to be all "cover" no "book". I truly believe the difference between owning a job and a business is catering. The difference between eking out a living and living a great life is catering.

Before I sold my interest in my restaurant at the end of 2006, I had built my sales to over three million dollars a year out of a hundred and four seat restaurant. Over a million dollars of those sales were in catering. Roughly two thirds from drop-off/self-service catering and a third from full service events.

Not only did catering contribute the lion's share to our profits, but each and every catering job was a free advertising opportunity for us. There's no other way to get paid to market your restaurant.

I learned this lesson the hard way. In the beginning, I trusted every short skirted, hot blonde ad rep. I bought tons of television, radio, magazine and newspaper ads. Unfortunately, they knew less than I did.

If my sales did not improve they'd advise, "You need to advertise longer. It takes time to build a brand." I didn't have the time or the bankroll of Coca-Cola or Nike to wait that long or to waste dollars reaching prospects across town that were never going to buy from me.

I learned to cater, not die! Catering is proactive, not reactive. You do not have to wait for a customer to walk in your front door. You can go to them. I catered many five figure events an hour or two outside of Nashville.

INTRODUCTION

Say what you want about his hair, but Donald Trump's Apprentice is one of the best shows on television for the entire family today. If you are in any type of business, each season offers up a mini-MBA on a silver platter with valuable lessons showcased each episode.

My kids, Jerrod and Jordyn, have no problem catching the moral and lesson each week. I remember an episode where two competing teams set up Outback Steakhouse concession stands at opposite ends of the Rutgers' campus before a football game. They were each given a space in the parking lot and then turned loose to get the word out about their stand.

The all male team was off to a fast start. They created an "Event" to draw in visitors. They were able to land an exclusive performance by the cheerleading and dance team at their venue. They were always a step ahead of the all female team when it came to promotions: getting flyers out, hitting fraternity row and the school's pep rally.

The women appeared doomed from the onset. When the concession stands opened, the line was long at the men's tent, and short at the women's. They started to get concerned. Well, if necessity is the mother of invention, then spiraling sales is the mother of out-of-the-box marketing.

CATER OR DIE

One of the women decided that if the customers weren't coming to the concession stand, they'd bring the concession stand to the customers. They loaded up aluminum pans and went to each tailgate party and sold nose to nose and toes to toes. Their booth was dead, but they humiliated the guys by selling 50% more than them.

Sort of reminds me of the first summer my barbecue restaurant was open. We had a concession stand in downtown Nashville for the 4th of July celebration.

We sucked wind. Jack Cawthon, a friend now, but not then, owned a little BBQ joint 50 feet away from us in the middle of all the action. He had an unfair advantage. Because of his beer permit, he was the only one selling beer on that sweltering July day. Made no difference how good my "Q" was, he had what people wanted, beer.

As a result, they bought their food at his place and sat outside on picnic benches polishing off cans of Bud and Miller Lite. He raked it in.

To salvage the event, we took trays, loaded them up with large Cokes and went into the crowd selling drinks like the hawkers at a baseball stadium. We never got rich, but it prevented the day from being a total massacre.

INTRODUCTION

What's this have to do with you and your restaurant? You can't always easily change your circumstances, like location or competition, but you can change how you look at your challenges. There are multiple profit and sales centers you can add to your restaurant (like catering, my specialty).

I have helped hundreds of restaurants keep their doors open. Layla Gambs comes to mind. A major road construction project was obstructing access to her restaurant. With sales down 28%, she was close to locking the doors for good. After hearing me speak in Phoenix, she rolled up her sleeves and started catering. Catering gave her the sales she desperately needed to stay in business and ultimately thrive when construction was completed.

She chose to cater, not die!

I believe we are at a time in the life cycle of restaurants where most operators are forced to add or expand their catering profit centers or risk going out of business. At minimum, failing to cater hampers your ability to make more than just a living.

I see franchises, chains and independents embracing the catering profit center. They all realize the potential to double profits without doubling overhead. Realistically, most concepts from ice cream to Italian restaurants can easily add ten percent to their top line sales. It is not uncommon to see twenty to thirty percent of a restaurant's sales in catering, but they must develop the systems to make it a reality.

This book is dedicated to helping you cater, not die. Within these pages you'll learn the same system responsible for me building a seven figure catering profit center. You'll see actual examples and learn real techniques from my archives; promotions responsible for building my catering sales.

The following pages are a transcript of a webinar I conducted with Frank D'Antona, owner of Cantina Mama Lucia. When he discovered me in 2003, he was doing very little catering. Due to his hard work and taking action on the ideas I handed him via my newsletter, educational systems and coaching groups, he currently is doing over sixteen times the catering business he was doing before me.

You will see a very detailed marketing flow chart of growing, servicing and retaining your catering business. As opposed to a book full of disconnected ideas, you will walk away with a plan you can use, step-by-step to build and better manage your catering profit center.

Lack of knowledge may be a reason for failing, but lack of trying is no excuse. After reading this book, you'll be armed with knowledge and asked to leave your excuses at the door.

Listen. Can you hear it? It's getting closer, ever louder. It's the sound of your competitors jumping on the catering bandwagon. Failing to lay your claim can be costly.

Now is the time to cater or die!

CHAPTER 1

NEW CATERING CUSTOMER ACQUISITION:

12 LOW COST STRATEGIES TO GET NEW CATERING CUSTOMERS

THE CATERING MARKETING FLOW CHART REVEALED

NEW CATERING CUSTOMER ACQUISITION

Michael: Hello everybody. This is Michael Attias, and I appreciate you all attending our webinar this evening, How I Built A Million Dollar Catering Business Out Of A 104 Seat Restaurant, My Million Dollar Marketing Flow Chart Revealed.

I have not revealed this marketing flow chart to anyone but my high paying coaching clients, but I'm going to do so now. I've got one of those clients on the phone with us right now, Frank D'Antono with Cantina Mamma Lucia. Are you there Frank?

Frank: Yes, Michael, good evening.

Michael: Hey, thanks for attending. I'm going to be turning to Frank to get some input from him throughout the evening. I'll let Frank give you a little bit of background about himself and his restaurant.

Frank, why don't you tell everybody how long we've been working together? You were one of my first newsletter subscribers, so tell everybody where you were before you got involved with my system, and where you're at now.

Frank: I think we've been together for almost eight years. My restaurant opened in 1989, but until we met, it was basically just dining room and carry out and very little catering. After we met, I purchased your material

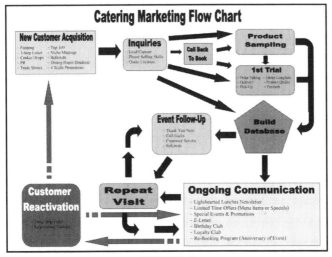

EXHIBIT 2

and dove in completely. Then I started using your system and our catering took off. It went from just a small percentage to almost 25% of my business right now. It's grown with tremendous potential.

Michael: Okay, so we're going to talk about a lot of these things right now. So, let's go ahead and jump into the Catering Marketing Flow Chart (Exhibit 2). I know many people are thinking, "Hey, this is a lot of information, and I don't know that I could do every single one of the things on here." What do you have to say to those folks?

Frank: Well, you don't need to do everything all at once. I didn't start doing everything all at once with the catering program. I gradually incorporated more functions as I went along. I still don't use everything, but the things that I do use are priceless right now. I don't know how I'd operate without them.

Michael: Right, so, it's sort of like going to a grocery store. You don't have to buy everything on the shelf, but there's something for everybody. You just need to get started with something because it's probably more than you're doing right now. So, let's go ahead and get started.

So, the first part of the Catering Marketing Flow Chart is new customer acquisition. That's what everybody is always focused on; how to get a new customer. So, we're going to start off with that, because it's the sexy thing everybody wants to talk about. It's not necessarily the most important, but it is important especially if you're just getting started building your catering business. So the first question you want answered is, "How do I get new customers in the door?"

FARMING:

HOW TO HOME GROW CATERING CUSTOMERS

NEW CATERING CUSTOMER ACQUISITION

The first new customer acquisition strategy is farming. Now, I'm not talking about farming as it relates to growing crops per se, unless you're talking about a money crop. What I'm referring to is the farming done by realtors, when they "farm" a neighborhood.

They will pick a neighborhood that they want to be the real estate agent everyone thinks of when buying or selling a home. To do that, every month, they'll send everyone in their "farm", the targeted neighborhood, a different marketing piece like a postcard, newsletter or flyer. By sending out something each month, the agent stays in front of his farm and are "top of mind" when they're ready for a realtor.

A "farm" for your catering business is no different. You first have to define the geographic boundaries that define your "farm". This could be as simple as a few blocks in a crowded downtown business district and as broad as an entire county or city. You'll then want to define the "who" or target market of your farm. In the case of trying to build corporate catering, you may want to rent a mailing list of all companies, churches and schools with twenty or more employees residing in the geographic area you defined. You now have a farming list to market to throughout the year.

To properly farm your catering market, you will want to send something a minimum of four times per year,

EXHIBIT 3

and probably up to ten or twelve times a year, depending on how aggressive you want to be. Your goal is that when a catering need arises for the decision makers in your farm, they think of you.

Some people in your farm may already have established relationships with caterers or restaurants that offer catering. Your goal there is to be "top of mind" when their first choice drops the ball, and they need a replacement.

An example of a farming piece I used at my restaurant is a simple full color flyer mailed via bulk mail advertising our catering packages (see Exhibit 3). Note: If you decide to send this flyer out three times a year, you'll save money by printing them all at once.

NEW CATERING CUSTOMER ACQUISITION

Keep in mind an investment in farming is a longer term strategy to niche marketing covered later in this book.

KISS COLD CALLING GOODBYE:

3 STEP LEAD GENERATION SYSTEM REVEALED

NEW CATERING CUSTOMER ACQUISITION

The next new customer acquisition strategy is what I call the "Three-Step Lead Generation System." Lead generation is defined as getting a catering prospect to raise their hand and say, "Hey! I'm interested in talking to you about catering."

As opposed to the cold call selling I was taught at my first sales job, lead generation brings qualified prospects to you that are already interested in what you have to offer. The three-step process was modeled off of collection letters. Each letter gets a little more urgent.

The premise of the letters is that we send out the first letter promoting a free sampling of our catering menu. The letter is a very simple black and white letter, printed on a laser printer, nothing fancy. We mail the letter in a #10, white envelope, hand addressed in blue ink with a live stamp applied a little crooked, Exhibit 4.

Our first goal is to get the letter opened. A hand ad-

100 Main Street
Nashville, TN 37027

Sue Jones
Shallwe, Cheatum & Howe, Attorneys At Law
100 Main Street
Nashville, TN 37027

EXHIBIT 4

100 Main Street
Nashville, TN 37027

2ND NOTICE

Sue Jones
Shallwe, Cheatum & Howe, Attorneys At Law
100 Main Street
Nashville, TN 37027

EXHIBIT 5

dressed envelope will peak everyone's curiosity. Once they open the envelope, the letter is designed to get them to raise their hand and request a free catering sampling.

If they didn't respond to the first letter, you send them an almost identical letter in the same envelope. This time you stamp "SECOND NOTICE" in red at the top of the letter and on the front of the envelope, Exhibit 5.

If they don't respond to the second letter, you send them a third with "THIRD & FINAL NOTICE" stamped in red at the top of the letter and on the envelope.

The theory behind three letters is you can take the response from letter number one, and you will get the same response from letters number two and three combined. For example, if you get a five percent response rate on the first letter, your second and third letter combined, sent to the same people with the same offer will equal that five percent. That's why you do three steps.

When I was using the Three-Step Lead Generation letters at Corky's, we were setting up appointments with twenty to forty percent of the prospects targeted. With traditional direct mail responses averaging a half to two percent, our returns were almost unheard of.

One of my clients and coaching members owns Logan Farms. They implemented our system as taught and used it pretty much exclusively to build their catering sales. After a year of using the three step lead generation letter, one store's catering sales were up 140 percent, and the other was up 500 percent. This is a very powerful way to build new catering sales.

COOKIE DROPS:

TRADING CALORIES FOR CATERING SALES

NEW CATERING CUSTOMER ACQUISITION

The third new customer acquisition technique is cookie drops. Frank, please feel free to chime in and talk about any of these techniques that have worked for you.

Frank: Yes, cookie drops we still do continuously.

Michael: Are you getting names for your database when you're out there calling on these offices?

Frank: Yes, I have a marketing girl who goes around to offices in our area. She collects all the data and we store it in our Restaurant Catering Systems database. If we're not successful right away in getting new business, we send the marketing material continuously. This keeps us in front of them.

Michael: I don't want to gloss over Frank's point. I have some clients who go out and make a lot of cookie drops. They then come back and tell me, "I went out, handed out cookies to over forty offices. It's been over a month and not one order. The point is not to hand out cookies. Imagine taking a girl out on a first date, showing her a great time and handing her a business card at the door and saying, "I've had a great time. Here's my business card. Call me if you ever want to get married."

It's preposterous to think you'll ever find a wife that way.

Catering prospects are no different. They need to be courted. There is that one in a hundred ready to book on the spot, but that's the exception, not the rule.

Four weeks after a cookie drop, you'll be forgotten. Once you find the right decision maker, you want to stay in front of them. At some point, they're going to be unhappy with who they're doing business with, or they're going to be ready for a change, and who are they going to call, someone in the yellow pages or somebody who brought them cookies and is staying in front of them once or twice a month? It's a no-brainer.

I publish an audio newsletter called Profit Points, and this month I interviewed a gal from Atlanta who has a catering company. Within four years she was doing close to a million dollars a year in catering. She primarily used cookie drops her first year to build her sales. After that, she lived off referrals. Now, she hardly does any prospecting at all.

Cookie drops are a great way to build catering sales. Who is going to be unhappy to see you when you show up at their office with cookies, brownies, mini-cannoli's or your specialty dessert?

THE POWER OF THE PRESS:

USING PR TO BUILD CATERING SALES

NEW CATERING CUSTOMER ACQUISITION

I want to throw PR, also known as public relations into the new catering customer acquisition mix. Getting written up in your local newspaper or mentioned on a popular local radio show gives you instant credibility. What the press says about you is far more credible than

---

For Release
Before Super Bowl Sunday 2000

For Further Information Contact:
Michael Attias
615-373-1020

Titan Super Bowl Appetites
Tamed With Tennessee Treats:

If the AFC championship game was any indication, Tennessee Titan fans will be setting new records for Super Bowl party food consumption. Corky's goes into red alert as they prepare for busiest barbecue day in history.

"We were slammed before the Titan/Jaguar game this past Sunday. We didn't expect the massive rush of people picking up football party food before the game," says Michael Attias, The Barbecue Evangelist at Corky's BBQ. "We had people shoulder to shoulder in the lobby waiting to get takeout, and the cars at our drive-thru were wrapped around the building."

Michael and his barbecue disciples are expecting a record-breaking day for the Titans Super Bowl debut. They have had to put their suppliers on stand bye and are bringing in their entire management team to handle the pre-Super Bowl party rush. Corky's has over six barbecue pits. They will be smoking round the clock to keep up with the demand.

"The Titans going to the Super Bowl is going to be bigger than Fourth of July," says Attias, "Early indications are fans could devour over 500-600 slabs of ribs and over 4500 pounds of bbq pork shoulder on game day."

To schedule an interview with Michael before Super Bowl Sunday passes you by or arrange to have a camera crew live on game day, please call 615-373-1020.

# # #

EXHIBIT 6

anything you could ever say.

Years ago when the Tennessee Titans were in the Super Bowl, we sent out a press release, Exhibit 6, about a Super Bowl catering package we were promoting. We were promoting a $9.99 rack attack for the Super Bowl. We ended up with a full color article at the top of the sports section, Exhibit 7, of the largest newspaper in Nashville talking about our promotion. You can't buy an ad at the top of any newspaper. It's not for sale. Normally, on our busiest rib day of the year, the Fourth of July, we sell about 400 slabs of ribs. With the press coverage about our Super Bowl promotion, we sold 800 slabs of ribs that Sunday. We ended up doubling our best day of the year by promoting ribs for catering a Super Bowl party. Besides the ribs, our customers ordered barbecued meats, sides, drummies and hot tamales. Never underestimate the power of the press in helping you promote your catering. You can start today by delivering some of your goodies to your local radio DJs.

EXHIBIT 7

43

TRADE SHOWS & BRIDAL SHOWS:

A ROOM FULL OF CATERING BUYERS

NEW CATERING CUSTOMER ACQUISITION

Any time you can promote your catering business to a room full of prospects and buyers, you leverage your time and energy. Trade Shows can range from a local business expo to a Chamber's business after hours event.

I have a client here in Nashville, Bar-B-Cutie, that I've seen at quite a few Chamber After Hours Events. They bring out samples of their best food, hand out business cards and catering menus and capture names for marketing purposes. They even sell catering.

Another type of trade show I love is bridal shows. First of all, it's an evergreen market; every year there's a new group of women getting married. They have a relatively large amount to spend on their weddings and rehearsal dinners. And they think they're only getting married once. So, if you do a good job, they're repeat customers.

All kidding aside, whether you're promoting a party room for wedding receptions or rehearsal dinners or rehearsal dinner catering or wedding reception catering, bridal shows are a great marketing venue. You get them all at one place at one time.

At the bridal shows, we took out a booth to promote rehearsal dinners. We created a banner with a strong headline to draw prospects; "Hassle-Free Rehearsal

EXHIBIT 8

Dinners". Exhibit 8 is a picture of our booth.

We handed out samples of our best food. You'd never put a new food item on your restaurant menu without sampling it first. Why would someone book a major event without sampling your food?

To capture names, we had the brides register for a free rehearsal dinner. As opposed to giving away a free TV set everyone would want, our rehearsal dinner giveaway only appealed to someone needing a rehearsal dinner.

If their rehearsal dinner is being held at a restaurant or a country club, they don't need what we're giving away. We don't need to waste marketing resources pursuing them. Anybody can register for a free TV set, but to

47

actually want your rehearsal dinner is a lot better.

Our rehearsal dinner registration form is designed to identify qualified catering prospects. Though we get great foot traffic and can even get a free list of all the brides attending, I am just interested in those brides willing and able to use me.

On average there are about a thousand brides at the show we did. We were able to generate about 200 qualified leads with our strategy. I can do five times as much marketing to a qualified bride, as opposed to mailing the entire attendee list once. By sending a targeted letter to the leads we generated, we were able to convert around ten percent of them into bookings.

THE TOP 100:

QUICKEST WAY
TO BUILD CATERING SALES

If building catering sales were "do or die", I would use a marketing concept called the Top 100. Chet Holmes introduced me to this concept. I think he called it the Star 100. You make a list of the top hundred companies you want using your catering services. You will want to target the hundred largest employers in your area.

It takes just as much effort to sell a catering for five hundred people as it does for 50. A company picnic for 500 is more lucrative than a catering for fifty. We rented a list of the 100 largest employees in middle Tennessee. Each month we pursued these companies religiously.

EXHIBIT 9

We invested as much as five dollars per prospect on a mailer. One time we sent a life sized cutout of a slab of ribs, Exhibit 9. We had the slabs cut out by hand. It made a large impression on our prospects. One prospect called me three years after the slab was mailed to her. She called to tell me she was so impressed, it has been on her office bookshelf this whole time. She ended up booking three caterings for golf tournaments her husband was hosting.

The first year we targeted our Top 100, we mailed a very simple letter. Exhibit 10 is the headline we used, "How to make sure your caterer makes you look like a hero." It's probably one of the most powerful direct mail letters I've ever written.

We followed up with some phone calls and kept them on our mailing list. Within nine months, I booked $45,000 worth of large events with my Top 100. If you were to look like the lifetime value of these Top 100 catering clients, we probably booked close to half a million dollars or more in catering in the fourteen plus years I owned my restaurant.

If your operation can handle these larger events, this could be the single most powerful way to get a large bump in your catering sales.

**How To Make <u>Sure</u> Your Caterer
Makes You Look Like A *Hero.***

Dear «EXECPREFX» «EXECLAST»

Next to public speaking, the biggest fear most people have is looking bad in front of their peers. When a caterer doesn't live up to your expectations, you open yourself up to looking bad in front of many people at «BUSNAME»

EXHIBIT 10

RICH DOCTORS DON'T LIE:

RICHES IN NICHES

NEW CATERING CUSTOMER ACQUISITION

I remember growing up in Memphis, Tennessee, being impressed by the wealth of just about every doctor I knew. They lived in large homes, drove Mercedes or Cadillacs, belonged to country clubs and took fancy vacations. Today, all doctors aren't so financially well off. The average family practice or pediatric doctor makes about $150,000 a year.

Though an impressive income for some, definitely not rich. If you take into consideration the numerous years in school and mountain of debt, a regular doctor isn't doing that well. So where's the money in medicine? The big bucks are made by the specialists; plastic surgeons, dermatologists, cardiac surgeons, etc.

In any business, the money is made by focusing on niches, not being a generalist. You can declare yourself a catering niche specialist by declaring yourself one.

Let's say you wanted to target the high schools and middle schools in your area to use you for their sports banquets. Exhibit 11 is the headline of the letter we sent to this niche.

Now let's imagine the same day a school receives this letter, they also receive a letter from a competitive caterer. Their message is not niched. They send out a generic mailer promoting "we're the best". They put bullet points on their piece: Specializing in weddings,

**How You Can Avoid The Ten Biggest Mistakes
Made Planning A Sports Banquet.**

EXHIBIT 11

office parties, social events, etc.

Which caterer has the advantage? The caterer who niches. Why? The have hit the right prospect, at the right time with the right message, the key to successfully profiting from niche marketing.

If the decision maker were to receive the letter represented by Exhibit 11, there's a far greater chance they'll think, "Wow. This letter came at just the right time. I have a sports banquet coming up in six weeks. I need to call these guys.

Now if they received the generic marketing piece from the other caterer, there's a far greater chance they will never make a connection between this caterer and their ability to cater sports banquets.

Sports banquets have between one hundred and three hundred guests. Book just a handful of sports banquets, and you're bringing in nice sum of catering dollars.

Time after time, I've hit home runs using niche marketing to build my catering business, as well as, my clients. Since you are often targeting small pockets of prospects, the cost is usually low; definitely lower than using mass media hoping the one in a million catering decision maker will see and respond to your generic offer.

There is also a stealth benefit to niche marketing. Your competition will have no idea what you're up to.

Just so you don't think I'm a one hit catering marketing wonder, let's discuss some of the forty plus catering niches we and our clients have targeted.

Come January through April 15th, many CPA firms

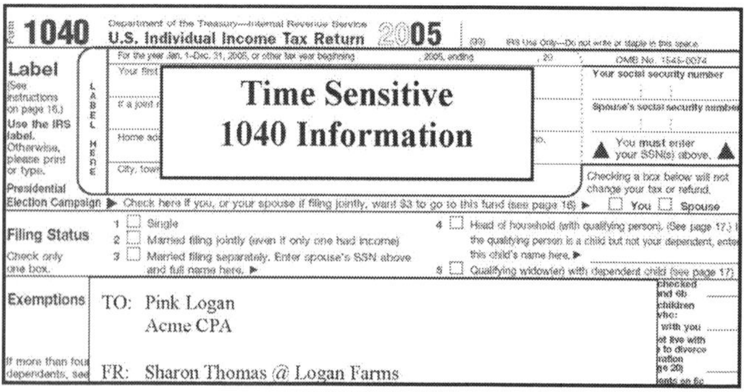
1040 U.S. Individual Income Tax Return 2005

Label

Presidential Election Campaign

Filing Status

Exemptions

Time Sensitive
1040 Information

TO: Pink Logan
Acme CPA

FR: Sharon Thomas @ Logan Farms

EXHIBIT 12

will be working nights and weekends to keep up with the backlog of tax returns due. Many of these firms cater in meals for their staff. Part of it is functional; they want their staff to stay in the office. Leaving to get lunch or dinner takes away valuable billable time. Part of it is motivational. If you must work after hours, you might as well get a nice meal for the inconvenience.

Exhibit 12 is part of a sales letter a client used to target CPA firms for this type of catering. They used the 1040 tax form as the background for the letter. The envelope was marked "Important Tax Document Enclosed". This will definitely get opened in a CPA firm. When you call to follow up, you'll have a great ice-breaker to discuss, "I'm the guy who sent you the 1040 tax return." Many of my clients have used this with great success. All of our clients have access to this and all of our over 500+ ad templates on our members-only website: www.RestaurantProfitPoint.com.

Earlier I mentioned evergreen niche markets. Here's one that can make your whole month of May; graduation parties. You can rent a list of parents of high school seniors and target them for graduation parties. Just about every family celebrates their child's graduation. Some will cook, some will book party rooms and others will use full service or drop off catering.

Exhibit 13 is part of a letter one of my clients used to

market his catering services to parents of high school seniors. The letter is written with a very emotional tone. He was able to tap in to the feelings a parent has for their child. He ended up with many graduation parties.

A rented mailing list isn't the only place to connect with this niche. I would approach your local schools and the PTA to promote your catering service to their parents. I would create a special graduation party offer, as well as, rebate a small percentage of all graduation party sales back to the school.

Though a little more difficult to target, many college graduates have parties to celebrate.

One of the first catering niches I targeted was Black Friday, the day after Thanksgiving and the busiest shopping day of the year. Let me tell you how I uncovered this niche. The first year we were in business, we were slow on the day after Thanksgiving except one large drop-off catering order from a retail store.

**Doesn't it seem like only yesterday
that your child was just learning how to walk......**

....and now in a few short months they will be graduating from High School. I have a daughter that will be graduating soon, so I know how you feel. No matter how grown up our child is, we can still remember like yesterday the way they smelled of Baby Wash after a nice warm bath, their beaming face as they ran into our arms as we came home from work, and that wonderful peacefulness when they would fall asleep against our chest. Time sure has flown by, and soon will be one of those last great moments that we can share with our child before they are "out on their own"....their high school graduation.

EXHIBIT 13

The light bulb went off, "Hey. If one retail store is ordering catering on the day after Thanksgiving, I bet they all are." The next year, we sent out a letter like Exhibit 14. I targeted forty five retail stores in my area and spent around $45 for printing and postage. That first year I booked over $6,000 worth of catering.

**Maximize Your Sales Volume
On The
Busiest Shopping Day
Of The Year!**

October 2, 2004

Dear «EXECPREFX» «EXECLAST»:

The day after Thanksgiving, November 24, is known as the busiest shopping day of the year. Retailers, like «BUSNAME», devote a lot of energy and money to successfully start the holiday shopping season off right!

EXHIBIT 14

Layla Gambs, one of my clients sent me a testimonial letter about what this letter I provided her did. The first year she sent out this letter, she spent almost $20 and brought back $6,800 sales. The second year, she spent about $38 on the letter, and brought back $18,000 in catering sales for Black Friday catering to retailers. Now this was in Phoenix, which is a large market. This works in any market that you have retailers, especially larger ones.

One of the questions that comes up the most in consulting and during seminars is how to best reach pharmaceutical reps. There are many ways to find them.

Our clients are given our proprietary system to get a list of every pharmaceutical rep in their city. Though more time consuming and costly, you can visit hospitals and medical offices and scout them out.

One of my favorite and most impactful mailer to pharmaceutical reps is Exhibit 15, my cough syrup bottle mailer. We mailed them a large cough syrup bottle with a sales letter rolled up and inserted into the cough syrup bottle. The letter was designed to look like a prescription slip. One of our clients, a Subway franchisee was able to do over $15,000 in catering sales to this niche in less than four months. If you do a great job for this highly demanding niche, you can build up a great base of repeat catering business.

EXHIBIT 15

One of the most effective methods our clients use to uncover catering niches is with a feature we have built into our catering software, Restaurant Catering Systems. We have an optional field at check out called "Event Type". Our system is preloaded with probably thirty or forty event types, but you can add your own event types.

Exhibit 16 is a screen shot of the drop down field. For instance, if one of your catering clients books a holiday party, a golf tournament, family reunion, company picnic, a church supper or any other specific type of event, you select that event type at the checkout. At the end of each quarter, you can generate a simple report from our catering software system to analyze your catering sales by event type, Exhibit 17. This will allow you to know what percentage of your catering business comes from each catering niche, and that allows you to go after other people just like it.

There's no need to beat your head up against the wall trying to figure out how to market your catering on a budget. The answers are right there in front of you. This report will lead you to two conclusions:

1. Which catering niches are we strongest with? You'll

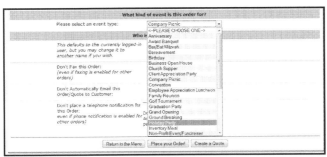

EXHIBIT 16

61

want to evaluate whether there's more untapped opportunity. You may decide to turn up the marketing efforts or keep them steady for this niche.

2. Which catering niches are you seeing some small catering activity that can be expanded. Let's imagine you discover last year you catered three golf tournaments valued at $4,200 in catering sales. I'm sure those weren't the only three golf tournaments in your town last year. If you believe it's a viable catering niche, you can focus some targeted resources to booking more golf tournaments.

Event Type	Corky's Nashville	
Holiday Party	$71,427.27	39.25%
Company Picnic	$52,501.74	28.85%
Golf Tournament	$24,758.73	13.60%
Bar/Bat Mitzvah	$9,556.82	5.25%
Church Supper	$6,230.32	3.42%
Sports Banquet	$3,178.16	1.75%
No Event Type	$2,712.78	1.49%
Teacher Appreciation Luncheon	$2,352.10	1.29%
Pharmaceutical Rep Lunch	$2,214.11	1.22%
Award Banquet	$1,441.41	0.79%
Client Appreciation Party	$1,430.57	0.79%
Other	$792.59	0.44%
Bereavement	$763.98	0.42%
Anniversary	$550.19	0.30%
Grand Opening	$527.03	0.29%
Inventory Meal	$474.50	0.26%
Birthday	$312.26	0.17%
Graduation Party	$297.13	0.16%
Employee Appreciation Luncheon	$147.25	0.08%
Tailgate Party	$107.80	0.06%
Non-Profit Event/Fundraiser	$107.40	0.06%
Office Luncheon	$104.90	0.06%

EXHIBIT 17

You could get a list of all the golf courses in your area. Find out which ones allow outside caterer and you now have a very tight niche to pursue. A quick Google search revealed there's an association for both golf course owners and superintendents.

It's this adopting of a catering niche mindset that was largely responsible for topping the million dollar a year in catering sales mark. So what are you waiting for?

REFERRALS:

TURNING YOUR CLIENTS INTO AN ARMY OF CATERING SALESPEOPLE

NEW CATERING CUSTOMER ACQUISITION

How many of your buying decisions have been made because of a friend's referral? Electronics, cars, movies, restaurants and vacation spots are just a small sampling of purchases you may have made because of a friend or trusted colleague. Personally, I've bought every single one of the aforementioned because of a referral.

I have a concept I call the credibility pyramid. At the bottom is advertising. What you say about yourself and your company is self serving and can raise the skeptical flag. What's written about you in the press is more credible. Even when the press has misquoted me, the benefits have been tremendous.

Now what your friends and trusted business colleagues say is just about the gospel truth in your mind. There are a couple of techniques to generate catering referrals.

The first is to ask. Later in this book we'll talk about how best to do that. Being a big believer in systems, I believe you should create a marketing system to regularly solicit catering referrals from your catering clients. Any time you can put any marketing system on auto-pilot, your time is freed up to pursue other money making and saving activities.

Our catering software, Restaurant Catering Systems, can be configured to actually send out marketing letters for you, like our Loyalty & Referral Program. We work with you to select the criteria to best reach your marketing goals. We actually print the letter in full color, fold it, stuff it, seal it, address it and put postage on it. It gets out the door without you lifting a finger.

Exhibit 18 is a copy of our Loyalty Club Welcome Letter. All of your marketing letters come with a custom letter head image, graphics and your signature. The purpose of this particular letter is to welcome one of your catering clients to your Loyalty & Referral Club. We'll talk about the loyalty club later on, but for now, let's focus on the referral component of this system.

Part of the benefits of the loyalty club is to earn gift certificates for the catering purchases made. We've taken the loyalty club and put it on steroids. It's modeled on the old MCI Friends and Family plan. This letter lets your catering client know they can earn a percentage of catering sales made by the friends, family and business colleagues referred to you. You can make the percentage anything you want. It can also be moved up or down for a specific client.

The letter explains the program and includes up to three offers they can pass on to their referrals. When the referral uses the offers, they get a special deal on their first catering order with you. Each offer has a tracking code keyed to the person making the referral.

EXHIBIT 18

This makes sure they get credit for all future referred sales.

By rewarding a referral, you increase your referral activity. I recommend sending out a referral type promotion to your catering clients quarterly.

USING YOUR DINING ROOM CUSTOMER DATABASE TO BUILD CATERING SALES

NEW CATERING CUSTOMER ACQUISITION

One of the benefits of being the number one expert on helping restaurants add and/or expand their catering business is I get hired to speak at many seminars, trade shows and conferences. Whether it's at the National Restaurant Association Show in Chicago, Pizza Expo in Vegas, The National BBQ Association Show or a Sysco House, I come across hundreds of operators. Not only do I have an opportunity to influence operators, but I learn a few things along the way.

Sadly, less than five percent of attendees of my marketing seminars, have a simple database of dining room clients in place. Though I could write volumes of how this database can help you build dining room sales, let's stick to its value for building catering sales.

Your best dining room customers frequent your restaurant and love your food. These are the highest probability catering prospects. When someone knows you, loves you and trusts you, they're open to buying more from you. Unfortunately, in this message overloaded society we live in, many of your dining room customers have no idea you cater. IF I come in every Friday for your fried fish lunch special, I may have no idea of the multitude of other services you offer.

You must educate your dining room customers to your catering offerings. One strategy is send them a direct mail piece promoting catering. There are certain times

There's No Blarney In This Offer...
Free Fudge-Nut Iced Brownies
For Your St. Patrick's Day Celebration
With Party Pack Purchase

In honor of St. Patrick's Day, Corky O'Pig has decided to give you his version of the Pot Of Gold. Order any of Corky's Party Packs starting at just $4.50 per guest and you'll get FREE Fudge-Nut Iced Brownies for each guest (95¢ value per guest).

$4.50 Basic Party Pack includes **Fresh Pulled Pork Shoulder** (enough for 1½ "Good Sized" sandwiches/guest), **Corky's Famous Baked Beans, Cole Slaw, Buns & BBQ Sauce** (sub about bbq beef/brisket or hand pulled bbq turkey breast substitution.)

With winter in our rear view mirrors, a St. Pat's lunch for your group is a perfect way to let them know you appreciate them. And they'll know you really care when you show up with FREE Fudge-Nut Iced Brownies that your boss, Mr. McScrooge, would never spring for.

So right now, before a leprechaun steals this card, pick up the phone and call Corky's at 615-373-1020 and order any Party Pack at $4.50 or greater and get FREE Fudge-Nut Iced Brownies for each guest (95¢ value per guest)!

Not Valid With Any Other Offer – Expires March 31, 2004 – Requires Party Pack purchase of at Least $4.50 Per Guest

INSERT
LOGO
HERE

100 Franklin Road
Brentwood, TN 37027

615-373-1020

EXHIBIT 19

of year individuals use a caterer for parties or family gatherings: Super Bowl, St. Patrick's Day, Graduations, Mother's Day, Memorial Day, Father's Day, Fourth of July, Labor Day, Tailgating, Halloween, Thanksgiving, Christmas, New Year's Eve and New Year's Day. Exhibit 19 is a St. Patrick's Day postcard we used at my restaurant. (Note: Many of the marketing piece examples you see are from my archives and reflect very low prices by today's standards.

Michael: Frank, how do you let your dining room customers know about your catering services.

Frank: Information is included in our dining room newsletter.

71

Michael: I've seen your newsletter. It's very well done and always has an ad or article promoting your catering. Kyle Agha, owner of New Town Bistro and Bar, and a long time client advertises catering in his newsletter as well. Exhibit 20 is a copy of the front of his dining room newsletter. It's a practically free way to get the word out about catering. You'll want to make sure your newsletter has some entertainment value as well. No one wants to read four pages of self-serving ads.

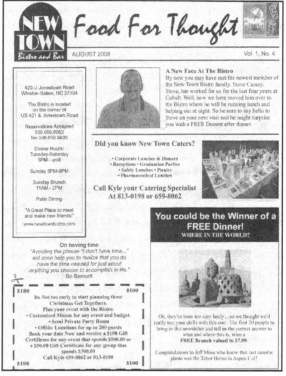

EXHIBIT 20

FOUR WALLS MARKETING:

THE LOW COST STRATEGY TO BUILD CATERING 24/7

Four walls marketing involves using your restaurant real estate to advertise to your current customers, as well as, drive by traffic. One of the simplest four walls marketing tools is the sign. Exhibit 21 is a picture of our drive thru window lane with a large sign positioned to get read while customers work their way to get their food. Four walls marketing plants seeds in your customer's mind. The more they are exposed to your message, the more it sticks, until one day they have a need for your catering and say, "Hey. Corky's caters. Let's give them a call."

Let's examine some other four walls marketing tools. Table signage, like Exhibit 22, or table tents are a great way to get your catering message out. We kept a sign like this on the walls of our booths year round to pro-

EXHIBIT 21

mote catering. During targeted seasons, we'd create catering table tents to promote using our catering service for a very specific niche like graduation parties.

EXHIBIT 22

Our hostess stand was a great place to advertise catering. We kept a flyer on display promoting catering, Exhibit 23. Repetition builds message retention. You can use internal signage like washroom signs for four walls marketing. Washroom signs are the most effective as you have your customer's undivided attention. They're not going anywhere until their business is done so to speak. I call it cereal box marketing. As a kid, we owned one TV set. It was black and white with no remote control and kept in our den. Every morning

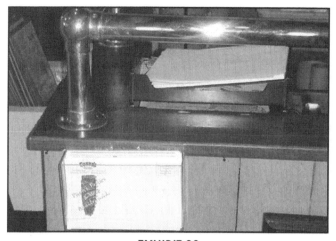

EXHIBIT 23

while eating cereal, I was bored, so I read every part of the cereal box from the entertaining back to the nutritional facts on the sides; with and without milk. Don't underestimate the power of a washroom sign.

A little known and used four walls marketing tactic is testimonial letters. We took all of our catering testimonial letters, framed them and placed them on the waiting area walls, Exhibit 24. These letters are not plain vanilla testimonials. Any time we heard great things about our catering, we asked for a testimonial letter. Your customers will love reading them while waiting for a table. The credibility of a third party endorsement is very powerful.

Some of my other favorite four walls marketing tools are: take-out bag stuffers, banners, buttons, receipt paper ads, bounce back certificates and message on hold recordings to name a few.

If words are more powerful than silence in promotion, a picture is even more valuable. To put the words "We Cater" on a sign is enhanced with a picture of a catering or a drop off catering. Unfortunately, a sign is two dimensional. Your customers may or may not pay attention to the message.

EXHIBIT 24

To really drive home the fact you offer catering, you must turn to a three dimensional catering display like Chick-fil-A uses, Exhibit 25. By placing plastic catering trays on display in their lobby with four color, cut out pictures of food as it looks at a catering, their customers form a stronger mental connection to the fact they cater.

EXHIBIT 25

You can easily emulate this idea with platters, bowls and chaffing dishes. These display areas are also a great place to showcase your catering menus. I have many clients also capturing catering prospect leads at these display tables.

So far, you've been exposed to some very powerful advertising and marketing templates. They are all available for download from our members-only site, RestaurantProfitPoint.com, most as Microsoft Publisher files. It is only a small fraction of the over 500 ad templates, ten marketing manuals, hundreds of hours of audio education and coaching call recordings, plus over seven years of back issues of my monthly marketing newsletter that gets mailed out in hard copy.

What's great about the templates on the site is they're in Publisher. All you have to do is download them and tweak them for your purposes; insert your logo, change a few words, print and profit.

Michael: Now, Frank, I know you invested in my Catering Magic System a long time ago, my original hardcopy course to show restaurants how to build and grow their own catering profit center. Do you remember what your investment was for the Catering Magic System?

Frank: About fifteen hundred dollars.

Michael: That's right, about fifteen hundred dollars. You can still go online to www.ezRestaurantMarketing. com and invest in that system for fifteen hundred dollars. But for Restaurant Catering System clients, they get a license to download and use everything in that fifteen hundred dollar system for free through RestaurantProfitPoint.com. Plus you get all of the extra materials, ads and newsletters we've created. In all, it's about $3,000 worth of blood, sweat and tears of not only what I've learned, but what people like Frank and other clients I've been working with over the past ten years have taught and continue to teach me. (NOTE: Later in this book you'll learn how to get all of these valuable catering building resources for free.)

Though there's way more than we can go over in this book, I want to share one other sales letter template that was a homerun for us. Hospital Week is when hospitals around the country recognize their nurses, doctors and their entire staff from the janitors to the head of the hospitals. We compiled a list of all the hospitals in our area and sent them a sales letter. Exhibit 26 is part of that letter. We used a black background with white lettering and printed it on transparency paper. When you hold it up, it looks just like an X-Ray. We sent it in an envelope with the words: "X-Ray Film, Do Not Bend" on the outside.

We ended up sending out about twenty letters, which cost us at the time maybe twenty to twenty-five dol-

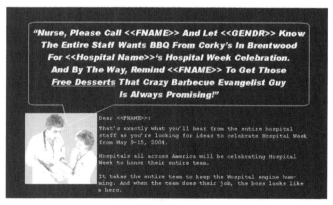

EXHIBIT 26

lars. This out-of-the-box creative catering promotion resulted in over $17,000 worth of catering bookings during Hospital Week.

Besides offering the first and only catering software designed for restaurants, we are dedicated to searching out and sharing the best ideas to build your catering business. We're always adding new ads and ideas to our members-only site.

SOCIAL MEDIA &
THE INTERNET

No book dealing with promoting catering would be complete without mentioning social media and the internet. This subject could be its own book, almost impossible to keep current. Though I'm available for consulting help in this area, let's examine some marketing ideas available via the internet.

1. A Catering Website: Hopefully you have a website for your restaurant. Many of my clients incorporate their catering business in their restaurant's web-site. Though this is better than nothing, you should have a dedicated catering website. You should link to it from your restaurant website and vice versa. Here are some ideas to incorporate, in no particular order or importance:

A. Your Catering Menu(s)

B. A Benefit Headline(s). Prospects want to know what you can do for them.

C. A Strong Call To Action. A free sampling, a free report and strong offer for first time catering customers are examples to test.

D. Method To Capture Names: What good is a website if you don't build a list of catering prospects to market to continuously?

E. Catering Quotes: Some of your catering prospects will want a low pressure way to get an idea of catering prices and packages.

F. Online Ordering: More and more corporate catering clients want the convenience of ordering catering on their timetable, thus avoiding telephone tag and busy signals.

G. Testimonials: Whether written or via video, this gives your catering business instant credibility.

H. A Blog: If you can publish relevant content, this could keep your clients and prospects coming back.

2. SEO, Search Engine Optimization: It does you no good to have a catering website if people can't find you. Search engines are the number one way people will be searching out your catering services. If you own a barbecue restaurant, does your name come up at the top of the search engines when someone types in barbecue catering, barbecue caterers or even the name of your city and barbecue caterer, Nashville barbecue caterer. SEO is an ever changing and complex subject, but here are a few things to take into consideration:

A. Targeting the right keywords to rank. Google has a great keyword suggestion tool.

B. Meta Tags, Descriptions, Keywords and Page Titles. If you're not familiar with these terms, they are embedded in your website code and read by the search engines to see how they should categorize you for searches.

C. Backlinks. These are links from other sites to yours. The more credible the links, the more credibility the search engines give you. Avoid paying for large numbers of low quality back links. A friend of mine, an attorney, hired a large company with credibility working with his industry to do his SEO work. He accidentally discovered they were using back links from pornography sites. He dropped them immediately.

D. Content That Gets Updated Constantly. A stale site gets passed over. Posting new blog entries makes you more favorable to search engines.

E. Social Media: Linking your website to and from your Facebook, Twitter and Linked In helps with SEO.

3. Online Reputation: Yelp, City Search and Urban Spoon are social media websites potential clients use to review restaurant, catering and other services. By monitoring your online reputation, you can solve any problems that come up. Encourage your clients to post favorable reviews, but never do it yourself as a "fake" person. Prospects can smell a dead fish miles away.

4. Social Media: Facebook pages are a great way for your catering customers to "Like" your catering business. Yes. You need a separate Facebook page for your catering profit center. Post pictures of your caterings to your Facebook page and share the link with your catering clients. Encourage them to share the link to their event photos with their employees, clients, members, etc. Twitter allows you to "tweet" messages to your followers. Linked In is the business to business social media. By posting you and your company on Linked In, you can connect with prospects, clients and peers.

5. Google Adwords: When you type "caterers" or any other search term into Google or other search engines, you will see ads at the top of the result, as well as, to the entire right side. Businesses bid for these ads. They only pay when an ad is clicked on, thus taking a prospect to their site. The more you are willing to pay, the higher you will rank on these paid ads. Google also takes into consideration your click through rate, or the percentage of people seeing your ad who click on it. The higher the click through rate, the higher the relevance. You are rewarded for this with a lower cost per click rate. Since you only pay for results, this is a low cost medium to test. Keep in mind you'll want to bid on key words for local searches like barbecue catering, as well as, nation wide searches like Nashville barbecue catering. Someone coming to your city and needing a caterer will use your city's name in their search. Someone in Nashville will only use the keyword. They're in the town already.

6. Other Cost Per Click Sites: Linked In, Facebook and YouTube all have advertising services similar to Google, a pay for performance model. As of this writing, I have clients testing ads with Linked In. Linked In allows you to target your catering ads by industry, job title, geography and specific company name. This is a potential dream come true for targeting businesses.

7. Email Marketing: Though we'll cover it a little more in depth later in this book, it is important to add an email communication once a month to your catering marketing mix. Important: never rent lists or harvest lists from the internet. The rule is simple. No permission. No email. You definitely don't want to get a reputation for being a spammer.

CHAPTER 2

WORKING WITH LEADS:

HOW TO BEST DEAL WITH CATERING PROSPECTS

LEAD CAPTURE:

YOU CAN'T SELL CATERING TO A GHOST

Hopefully you walked away with a lot of really great, high return, low cost strategies to bring in new catering customers. Not all recipients to your new catering customer acquisition strategies will end up booking immediately. Selling doesn't end once you meet a qualified catering prospect. This is when it starts. You must enter all of your qualified catering prospects into a database. You can use one like the one integrated into our RCS CRM, a database on steroids, Exhibit 27, or build your own. Either way this means all catering prospects into a database!

Whether you meet them at a Chamber event, they call you on the phone to ask about catering or you've met them knocking on doors doing cookie drops, they must be in a database. Let's look at it another way. Let's say you go to take out a girl on a first date. You want to make a good impression, so you shower up, put on a splash of cologne and your best suit. You show up with a bunch of flowers. You take her out for a romantic dinner.

And at the end of the night, you walk her to her door, give her a hug, and…hand her your business card and say, "Hey, I had a great time! Here's my card. Call me if you ever want to get married."

You think she'll ever marry you, let alone call you. No way Jose! No. You see all women just want to be court-

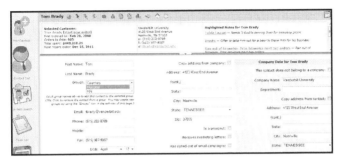

EXHIBIT 27

ed. They want you to put in a little effort. They want to feel special.

Your catering prospects are no different. You must stay in touch.

Michael: Frank, I'm assuming when your phone rings with someone asking about catering, you're doing the same thing?

Frank: Yes, we qualify the leads, and then we put all their information in the RCS CRM database.

Michael: The more information you have about your catering prospects, the better job marketing you can do. For instance, you may place your prospects into a certain group like "pharm reps". When appropriate, you can just send a letter, post card or email to all of your pharm rep catering prospects. This is called segmenting your list.

A lot of people think, "The job of advertising is to make a sale." Well, it is to make a sale. You spent all this money waiting for the phone to ring. If you can convert ten percent, twenty percent of those people that don't order on the spot down the road, that is a good investment of your marketing effort, But you can't always expect every single person is going to order right off the bat.

So, you've got to work those leads and keep them in the funnel. You're going to find that some of them are going to order a week from now. Some of them are going to order a month from now. I've even had people order three years down the road because they remembered my marketing and remembered me.

When the need is really strong, they will call you. It can be because the day comes they need a specific catering or menu you offer, or their primary caterer has dropped the ball. You want to be the one they remember. By staying in front of them each month, you will.

PHONE SELLING SCRIPTS:

THE WEAKEST LINK IN YOUR CATERING SALES CHAIN

You can spend all of the money in the world getting qualified catering prospects to call. Your phone can ring off the hook. But if the person answering the phone is not trained and qualified, you've just flushed all of your marketing dollars down the drain. This is not a place to save money or take shortcuts.

I had a client who was the franchisor for a small regional chain of restaurants. He brought me in to teach everyone how to market and sell catering. Some of his franchisees embraced catering and excelled. Others were clueless.

He hired me to mystery shop his franchisees. I played a red, hot catering prospect. One of his franchisees sounded a little unsure about what he could do for me. When I asked about getting the catering order delivered around noon, he hemmed and hawed.

"Well...noon is our busy time. I'm not sure if we can... (long pause)...ya (hesitantly), we can do that for you."

That's exactly what he said.

Now I'm not sure about you, but I would have absolutely zero confidence this guy could deliver. Catering is about more than good food. No one wants to be embarrassed. Again, it's very important that whoever is on the phone knows how to talk to customers. Using scripts as a training tool will help your phone staff do a better job answering questions and dealing with objections. Our clients have access to some catering phone scripts on our members-only website, RestaurantProfitPoint.com.

CREATING EASY QUOTES:

CATERING PROSPECTS NEED TO KNOW

Now some of your catering prospects will be happy to get a verbal catering quote. Others will need something in writing for them, a committee or their boss. Just about everyone will want to know what it's going to cost, before they make a commitment.

You definitely can create a spreadsheet or document template to make your own catering quotes easier to produce. Though necessary, the money is in closing catering business, not quoting it.

An automated quote creation system is something built into our catering software. We have an online quote creation tool you can link to from your catering website. Your catering clients and prospects simply go to our Create A Quote button, pick the menu they want, and then fill in information about their event and click on the menu items they desire.

What's great about having an automated quote creation tool, your prospects have a way to engage with your company without the pressure of speaking with a person. Some people like this as a first step to making a decision. They also love the ability to create a quote at their convenience.

Once a prospect has completed their desired menu, a copy of the quote is automatically emailed. At the exact same time, you are sent a copy of the quote as

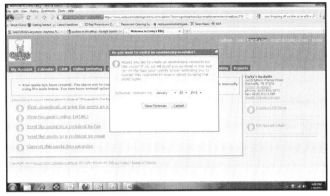

EXHIBIT 28

well. The prospect is in your CRM (database) and you can set a reminder to follow up. Exhibit 28 is our automatic quote reminder function. You have the ability to set a calendar reminder so the prospect does not fall through the cracks.

This is a great opportunity to build rapport and educate your prospects to some catering options they may have not taken into consideration. This positions you as a catering expert, not an order taker.

Whether you use a quote creation system like ours or develop your own, there are certain standard items you may wish to include like a cover letter, Exhibit 29, agreement language, testimonials from catering clients and of course a line item breakdown, Exhibit 30. By having a quote template, you're not having to recre-

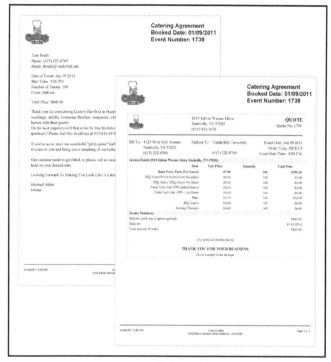

EXHIBIT 29 & 30

ate the wheel for each quote, send out a different one every single time and they get a copy of a breakdown of what they've ordered. So, it's automated the process.

Michael: Frank, why you don't tell me about how the create a quote feature is working for you. I know you used it extensively during Christmas, when it first came out.

Frank: It worked great. By getting the quote emailed to us, we can contact the people after the quote has been submitted to go over it with them. Nine out of ten quotes turned into orders.

Michael: So, that's phenomenal! So people came to your website, and they decided they didn't want to pick up the phone and ask questions. They just wanted to create their own quotes. So, that's amazing. You used our technology to do the selling for you.

Frank: A lot of our marketing materials are just to go online to get a free quote, and that drove a lot of customers over.

CALLING BACK
TO BOOK AN ORDER:

IT'S ALL ABOUT
THE FOLLOW UP

Michael: In my personal and professional life, I can't count the number of times someone I've called to get a price or quote from has not called me back to follow up on my purchasing decision. It's easily 75% or more of the time. What a shame it is to spend all of your money advertising to get someone to call to book a catering, and then the follow up ball is dropped. Whether you come up with your own reminder system or use the one in our system, Exhibit 31, it's critical to do so.

EXHIBIT 31

CHAPTER 3

SAMPLING:

THE WORLD'S OLDEST SALES TOOL

Remember the snake in the Garden of Eden? He had just completed his sales training course at the Devil's School of Soul Stealing, and Eve was his first prospect.

Fresh out of Selling 101, he pulled out the strongest weapon in his sale's arsenal: sampling. Yes, the snake temptingly dangled the apple in front of Eve and with one bite she was sold.

What is the lesson to learn from the world's first sales call?

Sampling, sampling, sampling!

When I was in second grade I sold the most chocolate covered almonds in my school with sampling. I bought the first box, rang the doorbell and offered my soon to be client a free sample.

Most of the time I sold a box or two. Why is sampling so powerful, and how can it help you increase catering sales?

The first reason is basic: you taste it, you like it and you buy it. Simple.

The law of reciprocation is the second. You do for me and I owe you one. I'm sure a certain percentage of adults felt obligated to purchase a box of chocolate covered almonds since I offered a gift.

If you're only motivation is to guilt people into choosing you for their catering by sampling, you won't get much business. Sampling has been responsible for booking many large events for me. It will work for you too.

I'm a big believer, if you've got someone who is willing to spend some money with you on catering, let them sample the food if they've never had it before. In fact, if I had a quote for anybody who had a hundred or more people, I would automatically ask them, "Have you tried our food before? Well, once you try it, you're going to love it. Would you like to come out to my restaurant with you and a couple of your committee people or have me bring you out a sample?"

I would always have them come sample either right at eleven when we opened and weren't busy. I could spend maybe twenty or thirty minutes with them answering questions, and then get back to work. My second suggested time was a late lunch; 1:30 or 2:00 in the afternoon when things slow down. I would also offer to come bring samples for them and their committee members.

Michael: Obviously, if your food sucks, this is not a good idea. You're not going to do anything but hurt yourself. Frank, do you use product sampling?

Frank: Mostly with the cookie drops when we qualify our prospects and they have a large enough work force. We automatically tell them we will bring food out when it's convenient for them.

Michael: I would imagine that works pretty well for you.

Frank: Yes, everybody wants a free meal.

Michael: Right, and obviously it sells itself. I've been to Frank's restaurant quite a few times, and he delivers. He's the real deal. He delivers really good food.

Often times, you're going to have a committee making the decision like a picnic or a holiday party committee. My favorite selling question is the magic wand question: "If I had a magic wand and could grant you one wish for this event what would it be?" You then want to shut up and listen.

Thanks to the magic wand question, one time I found out the committee was upset with another caterer who had run out of food at a party at the home of their company VP. We used this information to let them know and push home the fact we were the only caterer with a 120% guarantee. If we ran out of food, we'd give them their food for free and also give them 20% off their next event. This was what closed the deal. Keep in mind, this company was two hours away in Huntsville, Alabama. So, that shows you how strong the magic wand question can be.

Now, we'll talk about the first trial because up until now, we're just dealing with the prospect, and now they're not a customer – technically they are a customer, but you want to get them past that first trial so they're a repeat customer.

CHAPTER 4

THE FIRST CATERING TRIAL:

PUT YOUR BEST FOOT FORWARD

ORDER TAKING:

LOOK LIKE A PRO

THE FIRST CATERING TRIAL

How you take a catering order sets the stage for what people can expect from your company. In this age of computerization, you want to look like you run a professional organization.

Michael: I'm not going out on a big limb, Frank, but I'm going to guess before you invested in our catering software, all your orders were done by hand on paper. You had to ask new and repeat catering customers for their contact information each and every time. You probably had to ask for their credit card number each time, as well as, where's it was to be delivered with special instructions. Now, that your catering business is computerized, I bet you look a lot more professional when you go to take an order?

Frank: People love it! Yes. Of course, you know that Michael. We handwrote everything. And right now, I don't know how we survived doing it.

Michael: Whether you use a system like ours or not, you want to be thinking about two types of order taking. The first is online ordering. We have online ordering built into our system for free, but you're free to go find a standalone service to handle online ordering for anywhere between $25-$100 a month.

When looking for an online ordering system, a catering customer or prospect should be able to view your menu(s). Obviously, you want a system that will have the ability to upload pictures of your menu items. Color food photography sells your food much better than words on a screen.

A good online ordering system should also allow your customers and prospects to create their own quotes. It goes without saying, they should also be allowed to place online orders, review their order history and calendar. You'll also want the functionality to allow customers to place duplicate orders with a touch of a button. Everyone wants the convenience of logging in, ordering and going about the rest of their day.

Another feature I would demand in an online ordering system is an upsell module like Exhibit 32. You give up a certain amount of selling control when someone goes online to order. You don't have an opportunity to suggest complimentary items. Our system comes with an upsell module at no extra cost.

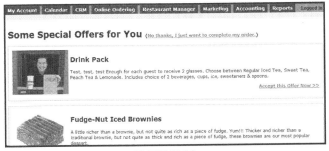

EXHIBIT 32

117

THE FIRST CATERING TRIAL

When a customer calls into your restaurant, you want to be able to pull up his contact record in a matter of seconds. In our CRM, when a contact's record appears, you can see some very important information about them, Exhibit 33: the first time they ordered, the last time they ordered, the number of times they've ordered, and the total dollars spent with you. You can also create highlighted notes. These are critical notes you want to see at all times when dealing with a catering client. Imagine one of your clients always needs a vegetarian dish. You'll look like a genius reminding them. What if the last order had a slight mishap, and you owe them dessert on this order. Again, you look like you run a company that stays on top of things. This level of customer service puts you light-years ahead of your competitors.

If you notice in Exhibit 33, you can get an order started immediately by hitting the "Start New Order" hyperlink. If you're going to computerize your catering business, it should be simple and powerful to use.

EXHIBIT 33

DELIVERIES:

HALF OF SUCCESS
IS SHOWING UP...ON TIME

THE FIRST CATERING TRIAL

One of the biggest kisses of death in catering is showing up late. It matters not how great your food or your catering crew, if you are late. The decision maker, especially in a corporate setting does not want to be embarrassed.

It's imperative you give yourself plenty of time to get to your final destination. Traffic is no excuse. Leave a little earlier if need be. One of the easiest ways to prevent being late, besides leaving on time, is having a good mapping system. When I first started catering, we bought Handy Maps. Even with a map, we still had challenges. Now thanks to Google maps it's easy to find where you're going. Google will even provide you with a street view for most addresses.

To save you time entering every "To" and "From" catering address, we have integrated with Google Maps. At a click of the mouse, your Google map appears with turn by turn directions, estimated travel time and map.

So, what you'll find is with Google maps, it will automatically put in your to and from address, so you never show up late.

Frank: Also, Michael, something that is very helpful for us is the delivery schedule built into your catering system. We print out a report the night before, so we can coordinate our drivers for our deliveries the following day.

Michael: Our Delivery Schedule Report, Exhibit 34, is designed to make coordinating multiple deliveries a breeze. You can set pick-up times and assign drivers. The report also comes with hyperlinks to the actual catering ticket, as well as, the Google map. This report can be emailed to your drivers and will contain the links, so they can review the ticket and map.

EXHIBIT 34

ORDER ACCURACY:
AVOIDING THE SECOND KISS OF DEATH

Whether it's a pick-up or drop-off order, you want to make sure the order is complete. Imagine driving thirty minutes to drop off an order and forgetting the mashed potatoes. This and worse has happened to me throughout the years. There are many ways to make it up to the customer, but it's far better to have a system in place to ensure it never happens.

One of the ways to do that is with proper reporting. You'll want to have reports to let everyone know what to produce. This not only goes for each order, but for

EXHIBITS 35 & 36

all the orders for the day. For instance, you may need ten pounds of fresh pulled pork shoulder for the Jones order at 11. All day long you'll need 121 pounds to fill all the orders on the book. Knowing this information in advance, helps prevent last minute runs to the store, or worse.

By having it computerized, either with a spreadsheet you build or included in our system, you'll reduce the chance of miscalculations. With the right system, it will make it easy for new staff members to help you plan.

Exhibits 35 & 36 are copies of individual production reports, as well as, a recap report for the day's production.

Another system important to making sure nothing gets left behind at your restaurant is what I call bagging labels, Exhibit 37. You can print out a sheet of these labels for each order. I use Avery 6-Up shipping labels. You can set up a template in Microsoft Word, or get them to automatically print out through our system.

As you start to assemble an order you mark on the labels what is in each bag or box. So in my example, box 1 has lasagna and breadsticks. I write that on the label and put 1 of ____ (leaving the blank until everything has been bagged). I then complete a label for the second label, third, fourth and so on. Once completely

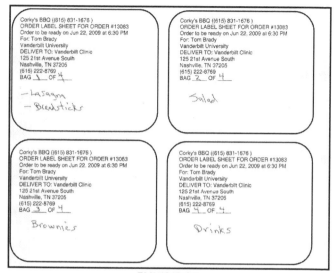

EXHIBIT 37

assembled, I count all of my bags or boxes and then fill in the blank line on each label. For this example, we have 1 of 4, 2 of 4, 3 of 4 and 4 of 4.

Regardless of which box is picked up first for this order, anyone can clearly see they had better be walking out the door with 4 bags or boxes. Not one more. Not one less.

Since we're talking about the order, let's touch on product quality. I can't stress enough, your food has to be good. If you're going to deliver hot food, make sure it gets there hot – cold food cold. They have insulated bags that you can buy that are sort of like pizza bags, that hold aluminum pans – half and full-sized aluminum pans that you can use for delivery, but aren't as heavy as an insulated container.

Now don't get confused by product quality meaning you have to use the absolute best. It's all about value proposition. Your product and service must be of highest quality for the price you charge. For instance, no one would expect a hamburger that sells for $1 at McDonald's to have to be the same quality as an $8.99 burger at Outback. In other words, your product must match what you're charging for the product. I think that's very important.

Michael: How you handle payments is a big deal for many catering clients. Do you do house charges, Frank?

Frank: Yes, we do. We use your accounting module to handle our invoicing, statements and collections.

Michael: This is probably one of my little secrets that most people really underestimate. Everybody takes cash, and a lot of people take checks and credit cards. Not a lot of people want to extend credit or do invoicing. We have invoices built in our system, Exhibit 38. Frank, why don't you tell me why you think it's important for your clients to be able to pay via invoices to get billed and pay later.

Frank: Like I said, we do mostly corporate catering.

Corky's BBQ
1015 Edwin Warner Drive
Nashville, TN 37205
(615) 831-1676

INVOICE
No.60829

Bill To:	Tom Brady	Deliver To: 100 21st Avenue South		Invoice Date: 12/31/2010
	Vanderbilt University	Nashville, TN 37205		Event Date: 04/01/2011
	4123 West End Avenue	(615) 222-8769		Order Type: DELIVERY
	Nashville, TN 37205			Event Start Time: 10:30 AM
	(615) 222-8769			Customer PO #:

Please Pay from this Invoice

Invoice Detail (1015 Edwin Warner Drive Nashville, TN 37205)

Item	Unit Price	Quantity	Total Price
Super Deluxe Party Pack [Per Guest]	$8.99	100	$899.00
BBQ Meat (Fresh Pulled Pork Shoulder)	$0.00	100	$0.00
BBQ Chicken (BBQ Sauce On Chicken)	$0.00	100	$0.00
BBQ Sauce (BBQ Sauce On Meat)	$0.00	100	$0.00
Rib Sauce (Wet Ribs (Sauced))	$0.00	100	$0.00
Party Pack Side (50% Baked Beans)	$0.00	100	$0.00
Party Pack Side (50% Cole Slaw)	$0.00	100	$0.00
Buns	$0.50	100	$50.00
BBQ Sauce	$0.00	100	$0.00
Serving Utensils	$0.00	100	$0.00
Watermelon [Per Slice]	$1.25	100	$125.00

Invoice Summary

Subtotal (with any coupons applied):	$1,074.00
Sales tax:	$0.00 [0%]
Delivery Fee	$10.00
Total amount of order:	$1,084.00
Total invoice amount:	**$1,084.00**
Total payments already applied:	**$0.00**
Total amount still due:	**$1,084.00**

THANK YOU FOR YOUR BUSINESS.

EXHIBIT 38

So, it's not the admin who is sending out the money. She has to send it along to the accounting department. So, they prefer it be sent in a monthly statement. It goes to the accounting department and they mail us a check each month.

Michael: Now, if you didn't offer a house charge, what do you think would happen to those clients?

Frank: They'd find somebody who did, or they wouldn't order as much. The whole thing that we try and stress is how easy it is to order from us. So, anytime we can make just going online and placing an order or picking up the phone and placing an order and not having to worry about all the little things, the more they're willing to do business with us.

Michael: Absolutely. We thought invoicing made a big difference in our business. As we move through our marketing flow chart, I must mention a database. In the beginning, we discussed putting catering prospects into your database. Once a customer places their first order, they should be automatically be moved to customer status. This allows you to segment your list for marketing purposes.

CHAPTER 5

EVENT FOLLOW UP:

THE KEY TO TURNING CATERING CUSTOMERS INTO CATERING CLIENTS

THANK YOU LETTERS:

MAKING A BIG IMPRESSION

Some people like to use the word customer and some like to use the word client. My definition of a customer is someone who has bought from you once. A client denotes someone of higher esteem; someone with whom you have a special relationship; someone who trusts you to take care of their repeat business.

Dan Kennedy, one of my marketing mentors says, "Most people think the purpose of a customer is to make a sale. The purpose of a sale is to make a customer (or in my words a client)."

It's important you follow-up with the client right after the event. The first thing you want to do is mail out a thank you note. Don't take a shortcut and send an email thank you note. About one in three emails get opened and read. It has less of a perceived value as an actual piece of mail. If someone spends two, three hundred dollars or more, aren't they worth a little over a buck to make a great impression?

When I had my restaurant, my office supervisor was in charge of getting the thank you notes out. It was hit and miss. I was always trying to stay on top of them. Mind you, in fourteen years I had four office supervisors. For some reason, everybody hates to get them out. At the end of a busy day, do you really have the time or energy to get them out?

Frank uses the Auto-Pilot Marketing built into our system to automatically mail out his thank you letters like Exhibit 39. He doesn't have to worry, "Did someone get the Thank You letters out?" Every letter uses variable data output. The system uses your custom designed four color graphical images within the letter.

Joseph, Thank You for Your Order

May 28, 2009

Joseph Beverly
Advent Associates, Inc.
Street Address Unknown
Not Available, NA 00000

Dear Joseph,

Just a quick note to say thank you for your recent order. You are a valued Corky's BBQ's customer, so we hope the food more than met your expectations.

We would love to hear from you either way, so we can duplicate our quality or correct any missteps. Please feel free to call me at (615) 831-1676 to speak with me personally or send me an email at results79@comcast.net.

You have many choices when it comes to your catering, but we are thrilled you make Corky's BBQ one of them.

We are always here for you,

Sincerely,

Michael Attias
Owner

EXHIBIT 39

You can use a simple logo, but most people have us design images incorporating their logo, colors and color food photography. It's totally branded for you.

We work with you to set the parameters. These parameters set triggers which allow the system to select which of your customers get a thank you letter. For instance, you determine how much a catering client has to spend to get a Thank You note. You can also select the frequency a note is sent to a single client; from no more than one a week to one a month.

Whether you use a system like www.RestaurantCateringSoftware.com, or do it yourself, you must send thank you letters out. Letting your clients know you appreciate them is a very nice touch. I guarantee you, 98 percent of the people you're competing with aren't doing this at all. It just takes doing something a little better than the rest to set you apart.

CATERING
CLIENT CALL BACKS:

REACH OUT
AND TOUCH SOMEONE

EVENT FOLLOW UP

The second strategy to follow up with a client after an event is a call back. Whether you pick up the phone after your lunch rush to check in with your lunch catering clients or first thing the next day, a real live voice makes a difference.

You'll want to call and ask how the event went. Solicit feedback, both good and bad, so you can improve your operation. If you identify a problem, do whatever is reasonable to fix the issue and make it right with your client. The money is not in one shot events, it is in building a herd of happy, repeat catering clients.

Whether you get a copy of the day's orders and use that to prompt you, or enter a call back reminder in a system like ours, it's important you are consistent with this.

A very successful caterer out of Atlanta taught me her call back formula. She called a client after the first, third, fifth and seventh orders. It was often enough to nurture a new customer, but not too often to appear burdensome. After seven orders, the relationship is well developed, so the client will have no problem calling if a problem arises.

CUSTOMER SERVICE:

IT AIN'T OVER
AFTER THE SALE

EVENT FOLLOW UP

If you've ever called a company you do business with, chances are their customer service department has your entire record at their fingertips. They know every time you ordered, what you ordered, how much you spent and can access any ticket. Often times they can pull up any notes on your account.

Whether you are the only person dealing with catering clients, have a salesperson, use your managers or any other combination, it's convenient and professional to have a client's entire record at your fingertips. You never want one person to be the keeper of this valuable information. If your salesperson leaves, you should be able to pick up the ball and run.

Catering clients, especially ones working for corporations want to deal with a professionally run catering operation. Know one wants to hear, "Sure I can get you a copy of that ticket from last year. I need to run down to the mini-storage and see if I can dig it up. It may take me a day or two."

How much nicer is it to hear, "Not a problem. Let me pull that right up. Here it is. The picnic you booked last June for 725 guests. If you'd like I can email the ticket to you right now. Are you still at Sue.Jones@ABCCorp.com? Great. It's on it's way. I'll call you back in thirty minutes to discuss rebooking the picnic for you."

EXHIBIT 40

Wow! Which of the caterers would you want to deal with? Professionals command a higher price. No one wants to work with a caterer who they don't have 100% confidence in. Looking professional builds confidence.

We built this level of total customer service into our CRM, our sales and customer service database on steroids. Exhibit 40 is a cutout of the client screen. Notice the little icons to the right of Tom Brady's name.

Each icon is a link to a different piece of data related to just this catering client. Here's an overview:

1. The Pie Chart: This takes you to the quick stats view so you can see an overview of their dollar value to you, place an order, see basic contact info and highlighted notes. If you look at the highlighted notes, you'll see an entry for "ran out of brownies, free brownies next time."

2. The Red Push Pin: This links you to a client's entire note history. You can add as many notes as you want.

3. The Green Push Pin: This takes you to all of the

to-do's scheduled for this client. A scheduled calendar item will show up on your calendar view. You can even set reminders.

4. The Phone Icon: This links to all of the phone calls you've scheduled or logged for a client. This comes in handy for any catering salespeople you have.

5. The Briefcase: This gives you a list of all the Auto-Pilot Marketing letters mailed through our system.

6. The Man: This takes you to a list of all meetings for a client, past, present and future.

7. The First Folded Paper: This links you to every catering ticket for a client. Once you pull up the ticket, you can create a repeat order, email a copy of the ticket out and see all relevant reports for that particular ticket.

8. The Second Folded Piece of Paper: This takes you to all of the catering quotes for this client. Once you pop up a quote, you can convert it into an order, print it, fax it or email it out.

9. The Bar Graph: This takes you to all of a client's invoices. You instantly see any unpaid invoices. You can accept payment, print, fax or email the invoice. This comes in handy when making collection calls.

10. The Gold Credit Card: Your client's credit cards are stored here. The cards are masked, but you can add, delete or change a card number or expiration date.

11. The House: This lists out every delivery address you have on file for a client. When taking orders, a list of all delivery addresses pops up. You can even add one on the fly. This link will show you every order delivered to a specific address. Imagine you have a pharmaceutical rep who delivers to a lot of different doctor's offices. You can instantly let her know what food was ordered at the last delivery. You even have a hyperlink to a Google map of the delivery address.

12. The Gold Folded Paper: This is a word processing tool. You can create a one page mail merged sales or customer service letter and have it automatically sent via the US Post Office to one contact, all members of a group, a look-up or your entire database. Once you approve the letter, we print, fold, stuff, address stamp and send the letter out. This is great for targeted promotions and keeping in front of clients.

Michael: So, Frank, what were you doing before you had all of this at your fingertips?

Frank: Hardly anything like this.

Michael: So, if somebody called you back—

Frank: Right, it happens a lot now. People say, "Do you remember what we ordered last Christmas for our party?" Now, it's at our fingertips.

Michael: What do you think the impact is on your relationship with your clients?

Frank: Oh, it's huge. People expect – now they compare us to other people, and they're like, "We never get this kind of service from other companies." We're the standard now that most other caterers in our area are compared against.

Michael: That's where you want to be. That's exactly where you want to be.

REFERRALS:

ENLISTING AN ARMY OF RECRUITERS

Let's talk about referrals again. When you call some-body back to follow up after an event, that's a great time to ask for a referral. You may ask, "Who else in your company do you know that could benefit from our service?" Remind them they will earn two percent of what the person referred spends.

Another trick I learned about referrals from my friend Hank Yost is to prime the referral pump. Often times a client may not be able to come up with a referral or two off the top of their head. He makes a list of the companies he wants to do business with. He gives this list to his client and asks them to review the list at their convenience and check off any companies at which they have a connection.

CHAPTER 6

OUT OF SIGHT, OUT OF MIND:

THE IMPORTANCE OF ONGOING CATERING CLIENT COMMUNICATION

CLIENT NEWSLETTERS:

STAYING TOP OF MIND

Not many people know I was born in Paris, France. My father was recruited by a U.S. company to move to Memphis for a job. At the ripe old age of two and a half, I came to this country. One of the first families my parents met had a son my age named Stephen. Stephen and I went to the same school through nursery school, elementary school, high school and college. In fact, it took us both five years to graduate from Memphis State.

Stephen went on to law school. Thankfully, I did not. For years Stephen has been asking me for ideas to build his law practice. One of the least expensive and most effective marketing strategies is a newsletter for clients. It's a great way to stay top of mind and educate them to your other offerings and promotions.

A few days ago Stephen was telling me about a casual acquaintance of his. From time to time, she would call him up with simple legal questions or need his help with a small traffic ticket. He's helped her on and off at no cost for around four years.

He recently ran into her and she told him about her boyfriend being in a bad car accident, Stephen's specialty. She wanted to refer him to Stephen, but couldn't find his contact information.

Obviously, Stephen was upset that after all of this free

LIGHTHEARTED LUNCHES

FROM YOUR FAVORITE CORPORATE CATERING SPECIALISTS AT MOE'S SOUTHWEST GRILL

July 2011

Sunday	Monday	Tuesday	Wednesday	Thursday	Friday	Saturday
					1	2
3	4	5	6	7	8	9
10	11	12	13	14	15	16
17	18	19	20	21	22	23
24	25	26	27	28	29	30
31						

The Lighter Side of 4 & 5 Year Olds

~ Melanie, 5, asked her Granny how old she was. Granny replied she was so old she didn't remember.

Melanie said, "Just look in the back of your pants. Mine say 5 to 6."

~ Brittany 4, had an earache and wanted a pain killer. She tried in vain to take the lid off the bottle. Her mother explained it was a child-proof cap.

Eyes wide with wonder, the little girl asked: "How does it know it's me?"

~ Susan 4, was drinking juice when she got the hiccups. "Please don't give me this juice again," she said. "It makes my teeth cough."

~ Marc, 5, was in bed and looking worried. When his mom asked what was troubling him, he replied, "I don't know what'll happen with this bed when I get married. How will my wife fit in?"

~ James, 4, was listening to a Bible

"Look on the bright side. With a credit score that low, nobody will dare steal our identities."

story. His dad read: "The man named Lot was warned to take his wife and flee out of the city, but his wife looked back and was turned to salt."

Concerned James asked: "What happened to the flea?"

~ Sunday prayer: " Dear Lord," the minister said, with arms extended toward heaven, "Without you, we are but dust."

The little girl turned to her dad and asked in her shrill 4-year-old voice, "Dad, what is butt dust?

Call Moe's Today for All Your Catering Needs!
888-663-7329

Or Visit Us Online at:
www.moes.com

EXHIBIT 41

legal work over the years, she didn't track him down. Without rubbing it too badly, I let Stephen know it was his fault. For years I've been telling him to send out a small client newsletter to stay top of mind. You never know when a friend has a legal problem. Stephen wants his clients to think of him first and make a referral.

Now I'm guessing Stephen still won't take my advice. You know what they say, "You're never a prophet in your own land."

Now if you want to profit from my advice, I suggest you create your own monthly catering newsletter. I like an oversized post card design. This allows you to create something that is a quick read. You probably don't have time to write and design a four page newsletter.

You'll want to avoid making your newsletter 100% self-serving. If you can throw in some entertainment, something your clients look forward to getting each month, you will have earned the right to promote your restaurant and catering business.

As part of our Auto-Pilot Marketing System, we design and license an oversized postcard newsletter. The postcard front, Exhibit 41, contains a top and bottom area custom branded for your business. You select the list, or subset of your client and prospect database, you want to receive the full color, glossy 8"x5" postcard each month. The postcards get mailed out automatically for you.

We license you different content each month. It includes a full color cartoon and jokes. Everyone looks forward to getting something funny in the mail. They'll share it with others in their office, too

Exhibit 42 is the mailing side of the postcard. It comes with a custom designed graphic. If you decide to promote an offer for the month, as in this graphic, you can have a large arrow highlighting it. You can also choose to not have an offer for the month or insert a custom jpeg the size of the offer box. This jpeg would be perfect for a custom message, picture or other promotional element. In the case of no offer or a custom graphic, the graphic at the top would automatically change to

EXHIBIT 42

153

not have a call out arrow.

The great thing about this Auto-Pilot Marketing promotion is you can set your parameters for the entire year and forget about it. Each month the newsletter gets printed, addressed and mailed with out you having to lift a finger.

LIMITED TIME OFFERS

A limited time offer is fairly self explanatory. Whenever you want to run a promotion for a limited time, this would be considered a limited time offer. It may be a special menu. For instance, at my restaurant we would run a special holiday catering menu from October through the end of the year.

We came up with this menu of smoked turkey, glazed ham, cornbread dressing, sweet potato casserole, green beans, cranberry relish and rolls as a way to get additional catering from our catering clients. Not everyone wants barbecue for each event. Around the holidays many employers would want to serve a traditional meal. By promoting it as limited, we were able to entice many of our clients into ordering our holiday meals. The group size ranged from a small ten guests to some large companies bringing us in for three shifts and over a thousand guests. You can never wait for guests to call you with new menu ideas. Anticipate what they may want, create it and promote it like crazy.

SPECIAL
PROMOTIONAL
EVENTS

Special Promotional Events are a perfect way to get in front of multiple catering decision makers at the same time to promote your catering. I have clients who have hosted Holiday Catering Open Houses to let their catering customers and prospects sample from their holiday catering menu.

I have one client, who after showing at a bridal show, invited his best leads to his restaurant for a special bridal tasting. It was a more intimate setting than the bridal show, and he could better showcase different meal options where the brides were 110% focused on him and his food. He booked quite a few weddings from this.

One of my most successful open house type of catering promotions was a Picnic Open House. We worked with non-competing companies going after the corporate picnic market; a picnic caterer (us), a high end campground facility, a company who provided giant inflatables and carnival games and a company who

---

Congratulations! You've Been Chosen To Attend The "Ultimate Company Picnic" Open House

Rain or Shine - You, Your Family & Selected Co-Workers Need To Reserve Saturday, March 23, 2002 From 1:00PM-5:00PM For A Day Of So Much Food & Fun You'll Never Want To Go Back To Work Again!

EXHIBIT 43

provided characters, face painters and balloon artists.

We rented a mailing list of companies who fit our criteria to book large picnics. We mailed them an invitation. Exhibit 43 is the headline from our sale letter. Each company also reached out to their client list who fit our criteria. This is a very powerful marketing strategy we used, the endorsement. By co-hosting the event, we gained instant credibility with our partners' client and they with ours.

Each partner in the open house brought their A game. We brought out fresh pulled pork shoulder, ribs grilled on site, fresh fried catfish and black angus burgers and kosher hot dogs grilled on site. For the decision makers and their families, it was like attending the ultimate company picnic.

A good tip about an open house is to get your primary food distributor to donate the food. It's good business for them, because the more picnics you book, the more food you'll buy from them.

Don't be shy to ask for this type of help. Your food distributor will just go back to the manufacturers and food brokers and get the food donated.

Making sure all of the picnic decision makers were thrilled really paid off. We ended up booking $20,000 in company picnics as a direct result of our first picnic open house. This doesn't even take into consideration the repeat business we garnered from these new clients.

E-LETTER:

MAKING AN
ELECTRONIC CONNECTION

OUT OF SIGHT OUT OF MIND

An E-Letter is an electronic newsletter. Just like it's important to send a snail mail catering newsletter, you should reinforce client communication via an email message like a newsletter or monthly promotion. Please don't make the mistake of overusing and abusing this permission based media.

Emailing once, no more than twice, a month is acceptable. Emailing two to three times a month makes you a pest. Clients and prospects will either delete your message without checking it out or opt out of your marketing altogether.

Our catering system has a built in email marketing module built in. You can send text and/or html messages via a WYSIWYG Editor (What You See Is What You Get). You have then option of sending the email to a single contact, selected contacts or a specific group in the CRM database. Exhibit 44 is a copy of a Thanksgiving promotion sent through our system by one of our clients. It is no accident that our clients doing the highest volume are the ones who consistently market to their catering clients and prospects.

Michael

From:	Joe Morley's BBQ & Catering [joe@joemorleys.com]
Sent:	Tuesday, November 09, 2010 2:49 AM
To:	results79@comcast.net
Subject:	Smoked Turkeys and Holiday Catering

JOE MORLEY'S BAR-B-QUE

Presenting our Fresh, Marinated, Smoked Turkey

Order for Thanksgiving from $39.99 to $119.99

Our poultry is delivered fresh, never frozen.
We then marinate our birds for 24 hours before
smoking over cherry wood for 6 hours at a very low heat.

Turkey only (from $39.99) served cold (for a *great* appetizer)
or hot for a complete meal with Baked Beans, Mashed Potatoes, Gravy,
Ranch Rolls, and a Mud Pie with Hot Fudge to serve 10-12 ($119.99)

EXHIBIT 44

CATERING CLIENT
BIRTHDAY CLUB

OUT OF SIGHT OUT OF MIND

I know a lot of restaurants, many my clients, who have databases of their dining room customers. I've been teaching this for years. One of the most popular promotions targeted to a dining room customer is the birthday club.

Each month you pull up and print a list of your customers celebrating a birthday. It is common to send a free meal to your restaurant, via post card or letter, along with birthday well wishes.

The redemption rate is high and the birthday boy or girl usually brings others to celebrate, thus making this promotion a money maker.

But why do so few restaurants use this winning promotion on their catering clients? On average a catering client spends more than a dining room customer. I can tell you personally, only one of my vendors and suppliers sends me a birthday card. It's Southwest Airlines.

Imagine how your best catering clients will feel when you send them a letter like Exhibit 45. To say, "Happy Birthday!" and give a ten, fifteen or twenty dollar gift certificate to a valued catering client has a big impact. Restaurant Catering Systems has this powerful marketing promotion built in. We help you word the letter, choose a birthday certificate amount proper for your establishment and set the buying criteria. For instance,

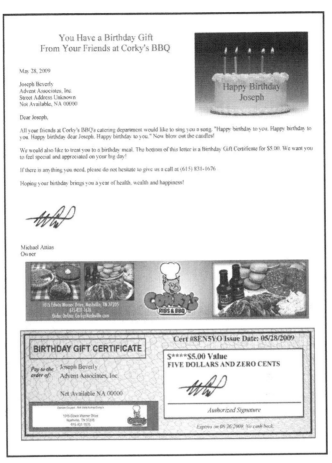

EXHIBIT 45

you may wish to only send birthday letters to catering clients who've spent at least $600 in the last twelve months.

So what's going to happen? Your catering clients will tell all of their friends and family members that you recognized their birthday. They're going to come in with friends and family to eat on their birthday. So, they're going to end up spending more money, and they're going to bring in people who might have never eaten with you before, which is free advertising. This type of marketing puts an iron cage of loyalty around your customers.

Michael: You're doing the birthday letter. Aren't you Frank?

Frank: Yes, we do.

Michael: How is that working for you?

Frank: Great. Yes, we get a lot of certificates back.

Michael: What kind of comments are you getting from these catering decision makers?

Frank: Well, it's just great that they come into the restaurant because most of the time, we're just dealing with them over the phone. So, bringing them into the restaurant not only opens them up to bring more customers into your dining room, but you're talking with them as they come in, which betters relationships.

LOYALTY CLUBS:

LOCKING IN
REPEAT CATERING BUSINESS

Loyalty Clubs have been around forever. I'm guessing the first one was a simple punch card. The airlines have been using loyalty programs like their frequent flyer clubs for years with great success. Personally, I fly Southwest Airlines whenever possible and carry two of their credit cards to convert personal and business purchases into miles. As a result each year I earn more tickets than I can use and have had a companion pass for years.

Years ago in my restaurant, we created a Pharm Rep Rebate Club. We gave 5% of a pharm rep's net purchase back in gift certificates. In those days, before this system was built, a manager would write the rebate on one of our business cards. I had one pharmaceutical rep who saved them up to pay for his family reunion.

All things being equal, a catering decision maker would rather do business with a company rewarding their patronage. There are many uses for these gift certificates from your restaurant: lunch, dining in your restaurant, bringing dinner home for the family and catering a personal party.

You definitely can adopt our version of the punch type loyalty program, but it adds more work to your already busy day. Our system will allow you to assign a percentage of all net catering sales to be rebated to your catering client. I have some clients giving away 5%

of the sale. The really aggressive operators are giving away 10% of the net catering sales. This is a great way to build market penetration quickly. I have seen some of my clients experience double digit catering sales growth by pushing our loyalty program.

I know a lot of people reading this are thinking, "Are you crazy? Somebody's going to spend a thousand dollars, and I'm going to give a hundred dollars in gift certificates?" Well, how much is that gift certificate costing you, thirty, forty dollars hard cost? Seventeen percent of them are probably going to go unredeemed. Chances are the gift certificate will be used to feed people who probably have never eaten with you before.

It has so many benefits. Let me tell you from what I'm seeing, a catering loyalty club will be a condition of doing business. More and more operators are jumping on

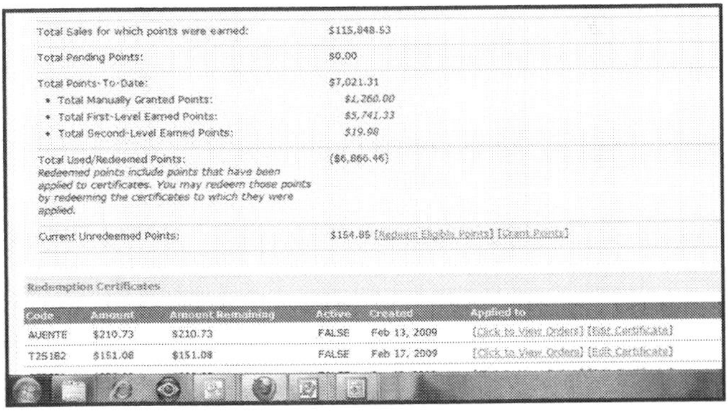

EXHIBIT 46

171

the bandwagon.

Exhibit 46 is a screen shot of what a catering client's loyalty page looks like. You can add and void certificates, as well as, see a line by line breakdown of all qualifying purchases.

Exhibit 47 is a copy of the Loyalty Club Awards letter that gets mailed to your catering client automatically. In our system you select the certificate color you want going out on your letter. You can even choose how many days you want until the certificate expires.

You also choose the dollar amount a client has to surpass to receive the certificate. It not only adds up their loyalty dollars earned, but those of people they've referred (discussed earlier in this book). Once all conditions are met, out goes the letter. The certificate code works in our catering system. If it is redeemed in the restaurant, you just go to our system and manually void the certificate. If they bring it into the dining room, you just manually take it out of the system.

I want to share a client testimonial I pulled off our website from Chris Smith, a Moe's Southwest Grill franchisee, who uses our loyalty and referral program: "Sales have greatly increased for us since we started using RCS. Our catering sales are up over twenty percent. We have one store, but in October had catering sales

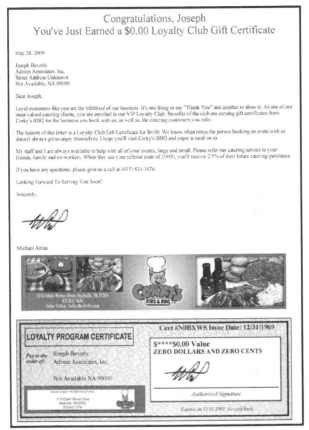

EXHIBIT 47

improvement greater than 56%, and other stores had 39% and my other store is up 26%."

His success is primarily because he is using our loyalty and referral program. So, I think this is some of the best marketing that you could spend your money on.

THE CATERING EVENT REBOOKING PROGRAM

OUT OF SIGHT OUT OF MIND

Half of all great marketing is common sense. I'm not sure if I learned the concept of a Rebooking Program from someone, or whether it was just a flash of the obvious.

At my restaurant, I spent quite a lot of time targeting and selling large catering events ranging from 250 guests to the thousands. There is nothing quite like walking out of an event knowing you took $5,000 or more to the bottom line. A great catering week for us put more money in our pockets than many operators make in a month. That's the power of catering.

I guess you could say it was my "catering cocaine"!

As mentioned earlier in this book, the real money in any business is in repeats. I wanted to make darn sure we did everything in our power to keep these large events year after year. Besides the obvious direct mail, newsletter and email follow-up, I made it a point to pick up the phone. If I had an event today, I would take a copy of the catering sheet and mark it to call the decision maker next year right before the decision is even considered. I placed the ticket in the correct slot of an expandable calendar file folder marked January - December.

Each month I would take out the catering sheets to call back. This marketing technique worked especially well.

The catering decision makers were impressed we were on top of things. Remember, the more confidence a catering client has in you and your company, the less likely a competitor can move in on your territory.

In hindsight, I should have used this technique for all events that could have resulted in a rebooked event. You have events that occur monthly, quarterly and yearly. However, using a manual system proved it a more daunting task.

Knowing how much extra catering revenue a Catering Event Rebooking Program could add without any

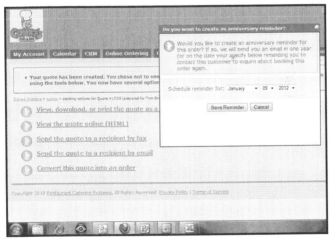

EXHIBIT 48

expense, I decided to make it a feature of our catering system. Exhibit 48 is a view of a reminder pop-up that appears after a catering order is placed in our system. This forces everyone on your team to make a conscious decision to either create a calendar reminder to rebook the event or not.

Exhibit 49 is a view of one of the four rebooking reminders available in our catering system. The reminder is placed on your calendar, you receive a pop-up on your screen, an email and can even receive a text reminder.

What a big shame it would be to spend so much time, energy and money to get a catering client to let them end up on someone else's profit and loss statement next year! Whether you use a system like ours or do it manually, this is something well worth the effort. In

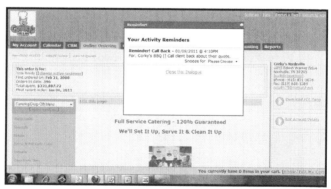

EXHIBIT 49

today's over stimulated environment, you can't afford to stay out of sight or out of mind.

Michael: By the way Frank, are you using this feature of our catering system?

Frank: Yeah, I tell all my guys to do that during the month of December when people are ordering their holiday parties. That's mostly for December, and then we set the reminder for late November. So, at the end of November the following year, we make all of our calls to remind people, and a lot of them rebook with us.

Michael: How did that work for you over the holidays?

Frank: It worked great. Almost everybody rebooked with us.

CATERING CLIENT REACTIVATION

Michael: So, now, we come to the point on the Catering Marketing Flow Chart where we've religiously been doing ongoing communication with our catering clients. Hopefully all of this will lead to repeat caterings. This is our ultimate goal to have this circle of repeat business. A client orders from you again, then you keep communicating, then they order from you again. In a perfect world, you just want that cycle to keep going on forever and ever.

However, sometimes that doesn't happen. So, you have to have a system in place to reactivate lost catering clients. For most operators,customer reactivation is reactive at worse.

One day the light bulb goes off, and they say, "You know, it's been a while since so and so ordered from us. What happened to them?"

That happens usually two to six months after they've ordered. It may be too late to get them back. Most of us don't have a memory good enough to remember each and every catering client who's fallen through the repeat ordering cracks.

Because you've spent all this time, effort and money to get this customer. The real money is not made on the first catering. It's made because of repeat catering clients. I would imagine Frank, what, twenty to thirty percent of your catering clients are heavy repeat users?

Frank: Oh, more than that.

Michael: That's where your money is made. It's off the repeat, not the guys who book with you once.

Frank: Sure, absolutely.

Michael: So it's imperative to have a system in place to identify and reach out to your inactive catering clients. On a very basic level,you could create a spreadsheet with all of your catering clients and update their last order date at the end of each day. Once a month you could sort the spreadsheet and reach out to anyone who hasn't ordered in 30, 45, 60 days or any time frame you feel is relevant to your business. You could reach out via mail or a phone call.

Though a catering client reactivation campaign can yield some of your highest returns, it's usually on the "Should" get done, not "Must" get done list.

To help our clients not lose clients, we've developed an auto-pilot four step customer reactivation campaign. The first step is to identify a time frame that a client steps into the inactive status.

Let's say if you haven't received an order in forty-five

days from a catering client, our system will automatically mail out the first, of up to three letters in a catering client reactivation letter sequence. Exhibit 50 is a copy of our first letter in the sequence. The letter can be worded any way you want.

We've found the best formula is to:

1. Let them know you're "Puzzled" they haven't ordered from you in a while.
2. The first reason you think could be the reason is "we did something to upset you".
3. If so, please call me to make it right.
4. If it's just because they've been too busy, enclosed are some special offers to get them back in the fold.

It's not very complicated, but it is important to mention both major reasons a client may have not re-ordered.

Now in our system, you can set up another two letters in the sequence for a total of three. So you may want the first letter to go out after 45 days of a client not ordering. The second letter can go out 20 days after the first letter if an order has not come in. You can send out the third and final letter 31 days after the second letter goes out. The beauty of this program, is it is on auto-pilot.

I don't believe in giving up after the three letters. At

EXHIBIT 50

this point it's a good idea to pick up the phone and reach out to your inactive catering clients who've failed to order after receiving three letters. To automate this for you, we've set up a report to fire off to your email, Exhibit 51, to let you know who has not responded to

Michael Attias

From: RCS System [noreply@restaurantcateringsystems.com]
Sent: Wednesday, July 01, 2009 4:15 AM
To: results79@comcast.net
Subject: This is your Customer Reactivation Report for Jul 01, 2009

Corky's BBQ

Your Customer Reactivation Report for Jul 01, 2009

This report shows all of your customers who have placed at least one order in the past 90 days, but who have not recently placed an order (inactive for at least 65 days).

Customer Name	Company Name	Last Ordered On	Total Gross Sales	View Customer Account
Ragan Anderson	Hospitality Control Solutions	04/09/2009	$1,501.36	View Customer Data
Howard Bender	Schmaltz's Deli	04/20/2009	$1,501.36	View Customer Data
Jason Burns	Puffy Muffin	04/06/2009	$1,501.36	View Customer Data
Tom Chapman	Subway Dallas	04/02/2009	$1,620.61	View Customer Data
Tom Elliott	Kona Bistro	04/13/2009	$1,618.04	View Customer Data
Peter Guy	Sysco Nashville	04/15/2009	$1,846.59	View Customer Data
Stephanie Mehta	Smiling Moose Deli	04/24/2009	$1,356.47	View Customer Data
Mehdi Rezaie	Murphy's Deli	04/21/2009	$1,501.36	View Customer Data
Sara Riggsby	Moe's Southwest Grill	04/03/2009	$1,501.36	View Customer Data
Chris Smith	Moe's Southwest Grill	04/09/2009	$1,501.36	View Customer Data
josh torrence	Default Company	04/21/2009	$237.82	View Customer Data

EXHIBIT 51

the reactivation letters.

This report is emailed out on the first day of the month following the sending of the last reactivation letter. What I have seen, is often times an upset client may have not wanted to pick up the phone, so a call from you is very timely and helpful. This gives you an opportunity to address and solve the problem.

The second situation I see is new catering decision makers. Looking at my report, let's say I called the first name on my list, Ragan Anderson with Hospitality Control Solutions. The receptionist lets me know Ragan is no longer with the company. Sue Jones has taken his place.

I now have an opportunity to reach out to Sue. I can try to have her out for lunch or bring her a sample lunch. While we meet, I can let her know "What We Can Do For Her!"

Again, most great marketing has nothing to do with fancy ads. It's just common sense systems you can have running over and over again, preferably on auto-pilot.

Michael: Now, Frank, did you want to chime in on this? You're using this.

Frank: Yes, we are, and it works great. The automation is wonderful, how the letters go out, and I call everybody on the list that I feel needs to be called, and I talk to them, and just getting all the information on why, if there is a problem, I understand what happened.

Let's try to make it better, and nobody falls through the cracks.

Michael: Can you give me some rough statistics? When you go make these calls, why are you finding people aren't reordering from you? What are some of the things you're hearing?

Frank: It's very seldom that it's a problem that they had with us. It's just mostly that they – it wasn't, they weren't ordering in that time period, or they cut back on their budget. Those times that there are corrections that we can make or if there's somebody new, those are the opportunities that we take to get them back in the fold.

Michael: So, you are finding that there are some new decision makers that are at the company and that's keeping them in. Are you successful at getting them to become catering clients?

Frank: Oh, sure because we'll offer to send out food. If they want to sample food, usually they don't need it, because the company has been ordering with us for a while. So, they'll still place another order, but if they need a sample or they need me to come out and talk to them, I can do all that.

CHAPTER 7

WHAT NEXT?

I want to talk about human psychology. People are motivated by two things. One is pleasure; more specifically gaining pleasure. Now, we think we would do anything to gain pleasure, but studies have found that's not true. The biggest motivator is avoidance of pain.

We've got to be in some kind of pain to make a change; the greater the pain, the greater the motivation to make a change. You may have read this book because you are just curious. You may be asking yourself, "What does this guy have up his sleeve? What am I going to learn?"

You may be saying to yourself, "You know what? I am unhappy with what the recession has done with my dining room business. I am unhappy with the amount of money I'm making. I need to make a change. I am just pissed off and ready to make a change." Or, "I'm doing a lot of catering, and I'm tired of it all falling on my shoulders."

I was talking to a restaurant owner last week, and he is doing a third of his restaurant business in catering. It's all managed with paper and pencil, but he's getting tired of having to do all of the "manual" labor.

Ultimately, you've got to be in some kind of pain to make a change, otherwise it's not going to work long term. I want you to take a second to think about one of my favorite quotes from Ben Franklin:

"The definition of insanity is doing the same thing over and over again, but expecting a different result."

If you're not satisfied with what's happened in the past twelve months in your business, you've got to be willing to do at least one thing differently. Otherwise, your next twelve months won't look much different than the last twelve months. Fact is, it'll probably get worse, if you're not working on improving.

Any time I've had big breakthroughs in my business, it was a direct result of doing at least one thing differently.

There's one piece of the puzzle that's missing from you realizing success, and that's **action**. You have to be willing to take action to make things happen. I know people who aren't as educated as everyone else; they aren't as talented and don't have the financial resources of others; however, all of these obstacles disappeared once they took action.

The successful don't make excuses. They make things happen. It's daily, consistent action that gets them to the top.

When I first opened my restaurant, I only had an hour

in the afternoon to devote to building my sales. Like losing weight, it's not brain surgery. It just takes consistent action!

Do You Want To Own A Restaurant Dependent On You or Systems?

All restaurants are dependent on either the owner or systems. I was talking with one of our clients from Lunchbox Express, and he has a friend who is a restaurant broker. They were talking about the value of a restaurant. He said, "A restaurant that is dependent on the owner, like owner operator and just about everything is the owner's responsibility, sells for about seventy percent of earnings."

So, if you're making $100,000, you're going to sell that restaurant for $70,000 on average. You may be able to get $100,000. But if you have a restaurant that is heavily dependent on systems, it will sell for two to five times earnings. So in this example, the restaurant might command a sales price in the $200,000 to $500,000 range. Think about how much equity you're going to build in your business by creating systems.

A Little Test...

Here's a little test to see if you are truly ready to start growing your business and using systems to help you.

1. Does your food and service suck? If you have bad food and service, you know it. Fix that before you work on expanding into catering, because all you'll do is put yourself out of business quicker.

2. Are you happy with owning a job? There are some people who are very happy going in, bussing tables, doing hourly jobs around their restaurant, and making whatever they make. They're very happy with that. If you're happy, then don't waste your time.

3. Does your staff decide the direction your restaurant takes? In other words, you're scared to do anything that will upset the staff. The analogy I use is back when point of sale systems came to be main stream, probably around the seventies or early eighties. The staff was probably bitching and moaning and complaining, "Oh, it's going to take us time. We're used to writing it by hand."

Now, you are hard pressed to find a restaurant using handwritten tickets. You have to decide who's going to run your business. Who's going to set the direction; your staff or you?

4. Are you an expert excuse maker? Is this what you say to yourself and others? "My town's too small. Nobody has any money. Nobody caters. There are too many competitors, etc., etc. etc."

My system has worked for lots of people – big markets, little markets. There is a catering niche for just about everybody. It's people who have the "Let's get it done" attitude and don't make excuses that make money.

5. Are you proactive or willing to be proactive to implement a catering system? I'm not referring to a full-time job. I'm just referring to an hour in the afternoon to start.

When I first started building my catering business, I used to go sit down after our lunch rush in the back corner booth and tell everyone to hold all calls and leave me alone. I'd work on my marketing for an hour every day and then success came. It snowballed into more success. Eventually I hired an operating partner to run the operation, so I could focus on sales and marketing.

If you're not a marketer, hire a college kid. Let them master these resources, or hire someone on staff that would love to do this.

6. Are you happy with the money you're making? Again, if you're 100% happy, there's nothing I or anyone else can do to help you. But I will tell you, no business sits still. You are either moving forward or backwards. Going backwards is not fun.

7. Are you about to go out of business? If you're about to go out of business, catering is not some quick fix magic bullet program. You've learned some powerful strategies to move the sales needle, but it's not an overnight fix. It does take some implementation, and you will see consistent results if you work consistently.

Final Question:
Why Is All Of This Important For You?

Why is catering and all of the marketing I shared in this book important for you? Well, for me, it's a quality of life issue. When I was around twelve years old, my father went bankrupt. It was very difficult because I couldn't ask my father for money. There was a lot of stress in our family. My parents were always fighting about money. I didn't have the money to do what other kids did.

It took me a while to get over this and get past it. To this day, the bankruptcy has shaped my life.

I didn't want my kids to go through that. I don't spoil my kids, but they don't live without. They don't have to worry.

Right after the bankruptcy, my father had to go cook donuts in the middle of the night for a local grocery store. He has been a great role model to me. He did what he needed to do to put food on the table, and get back on his feet.

Now he's doing very well.

Right after I was married and at a cross roads in my career, I was listening to some Anthony Robbins tapes. I was going through an exercise where he had me visualize my past, present and future.

The first future was one where I imagined my life turning out with the worst possible outcome. I visualized living in a trailer with my kids dirty on the floor and roaches crawling over them.

To me that visualization was real. Tears started to trickle down my face until they became a river of sobbing.

Then and there, I decided that I didn't want a life filled with money worries. That's why everything I've done in my life has been to avoid money problems.
I saw catering as sort of a magic bullet for me to build up my restaurant sales. Each catering job paid me to advertise my restaurant. It was a great way to make extra profits that I couldn't make in the dining room.

The ability to market and sell is the ultimate security for you and your family. Even in the great depression, there were people making money. Most of them were great marketers and salespeople.

What you've learned in this book is the foundation of a skill set no one can take away from you. If we ever work together, you'll be able to use our marketing system anywhere you go in life.

I don't know what drives you, but I can assure you increased profits will help get you there. Be it saving for your kid's college, supporting your parents in retirement, providing for your own retirement, or funding the lifestyle you want, learning how to increase sales and profits will help you get there.

I want to leave you where we started: "The definition of insanity is doing the same thing over and over again, but expecting a different result."

If you're happy with what you've accomplished and where you're headed, you don't need to do anything else. I hope you've learned a few things, and I want to thank you for reading this book.

If you're not happy with where your restaurant is or is headed and want to increase sales, build profits and systemize your operations, you're going to have to do at least one thing differently than you have done in the past.

Here Are Some Resources We Provide To Help Restaurant Owners, Caterers and Grocery Store Owners:

1. Consulting: If you want to either fly to Nashville or have me come to you, I am available for a very limited number of consulting assignments.

2. Coaching: I am currently running a Catering Coaching Group that meets monthly.

3. Educational Resources: We have a variety of tools to help you; marketing manuals, audio programs, marketing newsletters and a collection of over 500 ad templates ready for you to customize and use to build your catering sales. They are available both in hard copy or download (www.RestaurantProfitPoint.com).

4. Catering Menu Engineering: Most catering menus I see from my clients are in desperate need of repair. Their catering menu has complicated their lives and left thousands of dollars on the floor.

5. RCS Software: Our software is designed to be an all inclusive solution to help you nurture catering prospects and turn them into loyal, repeat catering clients. The software is easy to use, yet very powerful in helping you increase sales and handle all operational aspects of your catering profit center.

6. RCS Catering Plus: Over the years, many of our software clients have asked for additional resources and ongoing support. We offer a system that starts with professional design and creation of your catering menu and actual marketing pieces to fit your branding. We also include access to ongoing coaching, marketing help, newsletters and a license to use our marketing materials. For the operator looking for a short cut to build catering sales, this is an option worth exploring.

7. Lighthearted Lunches Catering Newsletter: If you are just interested in licensing our monthly turn-key catering newsletter postcard, we will make that service available to you.

8. Workshops: From time to time, I hold small workshops to help operators with their catering and marketing. Make sure you are a subscriber of our weekly Restaurant Marketing Minute to get notification of upcoming events. (You just need to opt in to any form on our main website; www.RestaurantCateringSoftware. com

Here Are Some Resources We Provide To Help Franchisors, Chains, Food Distributors and Restaurant Associations:

1. Speaking/Seminars: I am available for a limited number of speaking engagements for food shows, restaurant shows, franchise meetings and sales meetings. Please go to www.RestaurantCateringSoftware.com/seminars for a brief video and other resources.

2. Free Catering Webinars: I am available to conduct a variety of catering related webinars for your customers, franchisees or members.

3. Free Marketing Related Articles: With author's credits, we make our library of over 150 marketing and catering related articles available for you to reprint in your newsletters, magazines and websites.

4. One-On-One Marketing Consultations With Your Clients: In conjunction with a speaking engagement, I make myself available for a limited number of consultations with your members or clients. This can include dinner the night before an event.

5. RestaurantProfitPoint.com Licensing: If you are looking to provide your customers, members, salespeople, franchisees and/or managers with a virtual "Library of Congress" of marketing tools and templates, we offer licensing opportunities. This is a great resource to build catering sales, as well as, a perfect vehicle to help sales people gain a consultative advantage in the marketplace.

6. Turnkey Prospect/Client Monthly Newsletter Postcard Service: We have created a 5"x8" full color postcard newsletter called the Restaurant Marketing Minute. This is a perfect tool for a food distributor to stay "top of mind" with prospective customers. We can customize the design to fit your branding and colors. With our auto-pilot mailing service, each of your sales reps can have their picture and contact information printed on the cards going to their prospect list. This is an automated service to reduce labor on your part. The front of these postcards has plenty of room to present special offers and events from you or your manufacturers. Often time the full cost of the postcard and mailing will be absorbed by selling this space to different manufacturers.

Please direct all inquiries for the above services to:

Office Phone: 615-831-1676, fax me at 615-831-1389 or email Michael@RCSMailBox.com.

Thanks for investing your time reading Cater or Die!

I truly hope I have helped put you on the path to prosper with catering.

To You & Your Restaurant's Catering Success!

Michael Attias

16151230R00107

Made in the USA
Charleston, SC
07 December 2012